Joy of Living

By the same author

We human beings have only one life to live; then why not celebrate and enjoy it? All of us are born with valuable gifts to make our lives happy; but we hardly make use of their full potential. If only we realise this, all of us can enjoy life.

Our domain is the present. Let us allow ourselves to drift into the past, nor should we avoid the realities of the moment by thinking about the future. We know we cannot change the past, but we can ruin the present if we are not careful. So let us not squander the precious little lifetime given to us by feeling sorry for the past that never returns, or worrying about the future that is uncertain. Let us try to optimise joy in our lives by focusing on the here and now.

Joyful moments can make a lifetime of happiness; their memories can create a heaven on earth. Remember, we have only one chance to live the happy life of a unique human being; and nobody gets a second chance!

Then why not choose to live a joyful life, as long as we live!

Joy of Living

Prasanna Rao Bandela

Sterling Paperbacks

STERLING PAPERBACKS
An imprint of
Sterling Publishers (P) Ltd.
A-59, Okhla Industrial Area, Phase-II,
New Delhi-110020.
Tel: 26387070, 26386209; Fax: 91-11-26383788
E-mail: sterlingpublishers@airtelbroadband.in
ghai@nde.vsnl.net.in
www.sterlingpublishers.com

Joy of Living
© 2007, Prasanna Rao Bandela
ISBN 978-81-207-3565-1

All rights are reserved.
No part of this publication may be reproduced, stored in a retrieval system or transmitted, in any form or by any means, mechanical, photocopying, recording or otherwise, without prior written permission of the original publisher.

Printed and Published by Sterling Publishers Pvt. Ltd., New Delhi-110 020.

Dedicated to

my wonderful mother

Acknowledgements

This is a product of synergy of many people whose quotes I have used as heuristic devices to highlight the ideas expressed. I admire their wisdom and insight into the complexities of human life. I am greatly indebted to the publishers of *Reader's Digest*, as I had researched the old issues for the material required for this project and quoted them profusely.

I am thankful to late Dr E.G. Parameswaran Emeritus, Professor of Psychology, Osmania University, Hyderabad, for his encouragement.

I am grateful to my friends K.L. Narasimha Rao, CH.S. Madhava Rao and Noble Talari who stood behind me at every stage of this project and gave me invaluable suggestions.

I would also like to thank K. Rajni Kanth for his commendable work in preparing the manuscript.

I gratefully appreciate the love, understanding and support of my wife Dhimathi and my children Srikanth, Sridhar and Vandana.

Preface

This book is all about us. Even as you read this, you will realise that taking birth as a human being is in itself a great joy; the awareness of *being alive* is a greater joy; and the feeling that you are *still alive* to enjoy life, is the greatest joy in the world. Its theme is *Joie de Vivre*—the (supreme) joy of living. Its purpose is to help you live joyfully. It tells you to enjoy life while you have it, for it does not last long. This book may give a new meaning to your life.

A special feature of this book is its use of quotes as heuristic devices. It contains wise sayings, intelligent observations, clever perceptions, deep convictions—of people like you and me who lived before and those who are still living—that can profoundly impact your life. Call it a book of guidelines or suggestions or rules. Whatever you call it, whoever you are, wherever you are, you need some of them (maybe more), if you want to make the best of your life. These are only guidelines that leave the final option to you. If you so like, you can make your own Ten Commandments to guide your life. But, remember, if you obey all the rules you may miss the fun!

Life is not a dress rehearsal where you can afford to falter and correct later. Yes, we are talking about your life—the real life. Of course, you have a choice: you can either enjoy it or couldn't care less. Life is indeed pregnant with joy, full of it, in various forms. Remember, it's all yours if you so desire. If you discover the joy of life, you can make it a many splendoured heaven. Living can be a great fun, if you have a passion for it. Love to live joyfully and enjoy every moment of life.

You are blessed with the gift of human life that is full of surprises. But on one condition you are permitted to enjoy it for only *one* term. Nobody gets a second chance to savour life again! Remember, *nobody*. Then, why not make it wonderful by committing yourself to enjoying it? Realise that the only reason to live is to enjoy it. Do whatever you like; and live the way you want. Don't worry, there is plenty of time to be dead! Try to be happy and enjoy life as long as you live!

Enjoy reading. It would be wonderful if this helps you live a joyful life!

Hyderabad
August 17, 2007   *Prasanna Rao Bandela*

Contents

	Acknowledgements	vi
	Preface	vii
1.	Introduction: Discover the Joy of Living	1
2.	Live Here and Now: Adjust to the Changing World	17
3.	Accept Yourself: Realise Hidden Potential	33
4.	Take Care of Your Body: That Is Where You Live	49
5.	Share Life: Enjoy Warm Relationships	63
6.	Love What You Do: Enjoy Work	97
7.	Satisfy Your Needs: Enjoy What You Get	110
8.	Realise Dreams, Achieve Goals: Don't Forget to Enjoy the Endeavour	122
9.	Success and Failure Are Relative	147
10.	Be Happy: Living Is Joy Enough	175
11.	Keep Happy Memories Alive: Create Your Own Paradise	189
12.	Celebrate the Festival of Life: Enjoy While You Are Alive	197
	References	212

**Find ecstasy in life,
mere sense of living is joy enough.**

Emily Elizabeth Dickinson (1830-86)
US lyric poet, 'The New England mystic'.

Introduction: Discover the Joy of Living

> The giver of life gave it for happiness, not for wretchedness.
> *Thomas Jefferson (1743-1826)*
> 3rd US President

> We all want to be happy, and we are all going to die. You might say these are the only two unchallengeably true facts that apply to every human being on this planet.
> *William Boyd (1952 -)*
> British Novelist

Being alive is the grandest thing in the world; in itself it's a feeling of great joy. Being a human being, you deserve all the good things in life. The joy in this world is so abundant that there is something for everybody. Take your share and enjoy it. To live is to enjoy it. Wise King Solomon says, 'I know there is nothing good for man except to be happy and live the best of his life while he is alive.'

The Invisible Realities of Life

It is important to know what gifts and joys life offers. But before we explore ways and means of enjoying life, it is important to know some of the basic facts about human life.

Let us consider some invisible realities and try to understand their meaning and implications for a joyful living.

Reality of this world is what our mind constructs

We human beings are programmed to construct *reality* of the world with the help of our brain and senses. We see the world with human eyes. The world we live in—all that we see, hear, touch, smell, taste and feel—is something that is created by our mind. In other words, the world we know is essentially a mental construct. But many people do not appreciate the 'constructive nature' of our reality. You must open your eyes to this fact, so that you may create more than what is, and instill the world with new and greater meaning. Walking on the tight rope of reality is indeed an admirable balancing feat that ensures sane and joyful living.

'Man proposes, God disposes.' We use this proverb very often when things go wrong against our expectations. But the truth is, it is not God who does the mischief but *reality*. It is reality's way of warning us when we attempt foolish things because we try to do impossible things or attempt to do things without required means. There is no justification in saying that we are the victims of circumstances, society or people. Perhaps what we are experiencing is the result of doing things against reality. We must accept the responsibility of our experiences because we are the ones who created them. Once we accept reality, a great legion of options is at our command. Only then we can be in control of our destiny.

Nothing Is What It Seems: What We See Is Our Selective Perception

We live in a society overloaded with information. Personal needs and future dreams, family concerns, financial problems, work related issues, network of friends and relatives, phone calls, e-mails, reports, files, deadlines, demands and many more things are at the back of our mind. Our thinking tends to be wishful, our hopes and fears tend to influence our thoughts. All these things compete for our attention, whenever we think of anything.

Our mind seems to have overcome this problem by tuning out things of lesser importance, while concentrating on one or two important things at a time. Psychologists call this phenomenon as 'selective perception'. With the result, our perception becomes selective—that includes few things that come from our senses. This explains why our view of the world is subjective. Sensations brought in by our senses are interpreted by our mind in a meaningful way. When we recognise our sensations and give a meaningful label, they become our perceptions. What we see is what we get, and therefore the world we see is a subjective perception. That is, our idea of the world is what we see in a selective manner. Our idea of the world, is therefore subjective. Our perception is our only real knowledge. When we go beyond what is given by senses, and derive some more meaning by reasoning, we call it cognition and understanding. This is the beginning of our knowledge and wisdom.

But then there can be a gap between our perception and reality. As a result we seem to see things that do not really exist. That is the reason why reality appears to be different from our perceptions and expectations. Our conception of truth, then, is our truth but not the absolute truth. It is your duty to find out what it is. If you want to discover the truth about the universe, go ahead, try find it. But remember, whatever you discover that will be your version of truth, because nobody knows the absolute truth. No one can be sure about it.

Meaning of Anything Is What Our Mind Gives to It

Meaning of meaning is endless

Philosophers have written massive books on the 'meaning of meaning', they still continue to debate on the subject because it is endless. In *Measurement of Meaning,* psychologists C.E. Osgood, G.J. Suci and P.H. Tannenbaum explain that the meaning that we give to the words is of two types.

Denotative meaning relates to the meaning of common objects such as flower, table, computer. The meaning of these words is the *same* to everybody. As these words have common meaning, everybody understands them. This is the meaning we find in dictionaries.

On the other hand connotative meaning is subjective; it differs from individual to individual even though the object is the same. When we qualify nouns with adjectives, their meaning takes on a *subjective meaning*. Consider the examples: a *beautiful* flower, a *heavy* table, a *fast* computer. Words like 'beautiful' or 'ugly', 'right' or 'wrong', 'good' and 'bad' are *evaluative* adjectives. 'Heavy' and 'light', 'strong' and 'weak' are adjectives of *potency*. 'Fast' and 'slow' are adjectives of *activity*. Most adjectives fall into these groups. Using these bi-polar adjectives on a seven-point scale, Osgood, et al. developed a measuring instrument called Semantic Differential. They say that the sum of these ratings on any subject can give a measure of subjective meaning given by different individuals. The most important point is that we human beings like to see things differently and give our own *subjective meaning* which is different from that given by others.

Meaning of life is subjective

Life is such a mysterious force that nobody knows what it is. We really don't know where from it comes nor do we know where it goes when it leaves the body. Nobody knows the true meaning of life! Yet, Pope John Paul II says, 'Even in the frailty of the last hour, human life is never meaningless or useless.' Meaning of life is essentially subjective, but even the subjective meaning of meaning is endless. That is why both science and religion are in the same pursuit: *truth*—man's eternal quest for answers.

As we are the creators of our experience, the meaning of experience is completely our own, always subjective in nature. Since our life is made up of our experiences, the meaning we attribute to life is also ours—subjective in nature. Our conception of life seems to be a kind of subjective illusion. Keeping this in mind, American author Edgar Allan Poe says, 'All that we see or seem is but a dream within dream.' 'Rob the man of his life-illusion and you rob him of his happiness at the same stroke,' says Norwegian dramatist Henrik Ibsen.

Nobody knows the truth about life
Our experience is a mosaic of fact, confusion, misunderstanding and fantasy. Learning the distinctions will continue all through our life. Our knowledge is based on this kind of discerning and learning. It may shock many to know that beliefs about life are not necessarily the truth. 'When in doubt always tell the truth. Is not the truth, the truth?' asks Falstaff in Shakespeare's *Henry IV*. Truth is always doubtful because it may not be the absolute truth!. 'I have become convinced there is no one truth, nor two; there are often several truths... .', says journalist Peter Jennings of CBC. "One reason why we are struggling is that answers are not black and white. As a journalist and as a person, I want people to pay attention to the gray." We must realise that no one will be able to know the absolute truth, because life has multiple meanings.

Our knowledge about this world is based on what our senses gather from this world; but those sensations are not sufficient enough to arrive at a reasonable meaning. We invariably fall back upon our experience to help us; but unfortunately our experience is very limited. As a last resort, we depend on our mind's intuitive powers that can make a lot of assumptions, axioms, guesses and beliefs about this world. Yes, our beliefs begin when our reason fails. That is why there are no limits to our beliefs, whereas our knowledge is limited. Look at the concepts like *gods, devils, angels, heaven, hell*. We have no knowledge about these things; what all we have are our strong beliefs about them. And the truth is, we don't know much about them. On the other hand, science also begins with beliefs, but no hypothesis is taken as truth unless it is verified by experiments.

As we keep guessing, our assumptions about life in the universe keep multiplying. That is perhaps one reason why Austrian scientist Konrad Lorenz suggests that, " It is a good morning exercise for a research scientist to discard a pet hypothesis every day before breakfast." When you make a guess about any unknown thing, you will soon discard it when you make another one. That is because nobody knows the truth about life or the universe.

We don't know if we really know what we think we know. That is the true nature of our knowledge. "There are known knowns—there are things we know we know," says Donald Rumsfeld, US Defence Secretary. "We also know that there are known unknowns—that is to say we know there are some things we do not know. But there are also unknown unknowns—the ones we do not know." It is the challenge of the unknown that prompts man to explore the world. We must accept the fact that there are hidden truths about the life we live ; because we don't know all that is out there. Once you appreciate that no one will be able to know the absolute truth, you will admire life with all its promises and limitations.

Human life is but a moment in the eternal stream of time
"When we are mindful of every nuance of our natural world we finally get the picture that we are only given one dazzling moment of life here on earth, and must stand before that reality both humble and elevated, subject to every law of the universe and grateful for our brief but intrinsic participation in it," says American novelist Elizabeth Gilbert. Yes, our life-time is but a minute moment in the stream of eternal time. We must respect the short span of our life-time and make the best of it to enjoy life.

Man is a finite being in the infinite space

"Man can will nothing, unless he has first understood that he must count on no one but himself; that he is alone, abandoned on earth in the midst of his infinite responsibilities, without help, with no other aim than the one he sets himself, with no other destiny than the one he forges for himself on this earth," says the French philosopher Jean-Paul Sartre. We humans are finite beings in the vast expanse of infinite space. We are given tiny bits of space and time to live the life of a human being. We are responsible for our lives. What we make out of it is up to us. Joy and suffering are our making.

Life is a miracle

No wonder, the origin of life on earth itself is a miraculous exception in the entire universe. And in the 15 billion years of cosmic evolution, the accidental appearance of man is indeed an awesome wonder beyond the comprehension of any human mind. "There are only two ways to life. One is as if everything is a miracle, the other is as though nothing is a miracle," says philosopher Albert Einstein. "Each moment of life is a miracle and mystery," observes British evolutionist H.G. Wells. Composer Arthur Rubinstein says, " To be alive, to be able to see, to walk, it's all a miracle. I have adopted the technique of living life from miracle to miracle." Yes, life is indeed more than beautiful, a little like mystery, a little like wonder, a lot like a miracle. It baffles every living soul!

Death is inevitable

"The meaning of life is that it stops," says a German philosopher Franz Kafka. The inevitable death is as casual, and often as unexpected as birth. " No fire, no heroism, no intensity of thought can preserve an individual beyond grave," observes British philosopher Bertrand Russell. Even the doctors can't stop death; they may prolong it for a while though. No one can do anything about it except accepting the fact that we are all going to die one day. Yes, one tragedy in life is its brevity.

But none of us like to think about the inevitability of aging or dying. And no one wants to die, though everybody will. Remember, the day you are born you are sentenced to death. The countdown began the moment you are born. You don't know when your life ends; it is only a matter of time. And that is the bitter truth no one can afford to forget. As the Greek philosopher Epicurus says, "Death does not concern us, because as long as we exist, death is not here. And when it does come we no longer exist."

Actually death is not something to fear about, because it happens to everybody. "You cannot conquer death but you can conquer the fear of it," says American author Elizabeth Coatsworth. Yet the very word 'death' is something that makes us sit up and take a serious look at our life. Whenever we see someone dying we express our condolences; it makes us realise that one day we also will die. But the fascinating counterpoint is our awareness that we are still alive—to enjoy life. It prompts us to make haste to do all the things we wanted to do before we end this mortal life; and the constant wish is to live as joyfully as we can while we are alive.

Many people believe that death is only a gateway to the life beyond. People love to describe it in glorious terms of high sounding words, such as *God's kingdom, heaven, immortal life*. But this hope of another life is but a mere belief. Since nobody knows about these things, they remain elusive. God-men tell us a lot of things about the life beyond, as if they have come back after death. They preach different ways of reaching out to life beyond and some people believe them; and in the process gullible people get exploited. On the other hand there are some people who pretend to be believers, because it makes them accepted in the society. The whole problem with some of them is that they don't know how to enjoy life on earth, yet they hope to enjoy afterlife. If it is there, probably they will do the same thing in afterlife — keep looking for joy somewhere else, while not enjoying what they have, because old habits die hard.

But the tragedy of life is not that it ends soon but that we wait so long to begin it. Remember, since there is plenty of time to be dead, one has more time to do what one wants. So, let us do what we can, to enjoy life. "Life is really short and its important to live colourfully," says Joy Rose, the founder of Housewives on Prozac. Yes, it is true, our life on earth is very short. It is important to realise this if we want to live joyfully. A Scottish proverb says, "Be happy while you are living, for you are long time dead."

Yet, life goes on ... till it stops
"In three words I can sum up everything I have learned about life: it goes on," says American poet Robert Frost. Yes, human life on earth seems like a never ending process, as one life ends another begins. Men may come and men may go but it goes on. It is likely to continue for some more time unless terminated either by the folly of man or by the caprices of nature as it happened to dinosaurs long ago.

"It is not how many years we live, but rather what we do with them," says General Evangeline Cory Booth of Salvation Army. We are given tiny bits of space and time in our life; that's what we have to think about, and do whatever we can within the time allotted to us. Of course it is up to us, how we choose to live. Life reveals its secrets to one person at a time. It is for you to find them. Your life is what you do in your life. You are free to live according to your own values—at your own terms. That is, you are free to choose your own destiny. Well, you are lucky as life is still going on. Get set and go. Life is waiting for you!

Life is full of surprises

We may love to bask in the morning sun and revel in its warmth, but we don't know what it burns. We may enjoy the tingling cool breeze for a while, but we don't know when it will turn into a fierce whirlwind or a devastating tornado. A walk on the beautiful beach may be exhilarating and a dip in the sea rejuvenating, but we don't know when the tide will bring sky-rising fatal waves. Dancing rhythm of swaying grass may be quite pleasing, but we don't know when the famine will strike the green fields. A joy ride on the roller coaster of life may be thrilling at every climb, exciting at every fall; but we don't know what danger lurks in the unexpected corner. Yes, life on earth is profoundly uncertain and anything may happen at any time. But you don't have to worry, because you are fully equipped to work out your own survival.

You don't know when you will fall in love or who will be your spouse. You may experience the bliss of a loving relationship, but you don't know how long it will last. Nor do you know how long you and your partner will live. You may bring up your children with all good intentions, but you don't know what specimens they will turn out to be. You don't know what stranger will become your friend in need; and when a trusted friend will betray you. Solid support of relatives may be quite reassuring, but you don't know what vicious thoughts are hiding behind some of those insincere smiles. Remember, there are no welcomes in this man-cheat-man-world. Surely, you will somehow learn to adjust to it in your own way.

Life may appear like a box of chocolates, but you don't know what you are going to get. You may be pleased with what you do, but don't know why you need other's approval or recognition. A position of power can go instantly like the air in a punctured tube, but you don't know why people cling to it . Money is only a means to buy goods and services but you don't know why people are obsessed with it. You can live within your means but you don't know why people want to acquire more. You can be happy with what you have, but you don't know why happiness eludes us. Sooner or later wisdom will dawn on you.

"This is the most imperfect world, true, but it has its virtues, and these you must find," says Maxwell Maltz, the psycho-cybernetics guru. " It has its good values, these you must find. It has your self, and this you must find." Life may look vibrant and volatile, yet it has an invisible dimension that fulfils your desires and aspirations. These you must explore. It is indeed an exciting adventure that unfolds while taking you with it. You may not have seen anything like this before. Yes, this is your life, full of surprises! How you balance it is all that matters—for a joyful living.

Life is a gift with a promise of joy
"Every gift from a friend is a wish for your happiness," reminds a well-known American author Richard Bach. In the same sense, if life is a gift to you, it is given with a wish to make you happy. Yes, there is a promise of joy behind every life. " The giver of life gave it for happiness, not for wretchedness," says former US President Thomas Jefferson. It is up to the receiver of the gift (you) to enjoy it or throw it to the winds.

Life is made up of choices: we make our destiny
Whatever we do in life, be it solving problems or getting things done, it is to please ourselves and be happy. Most of the things we do in life are either actions or reactions. They are, in fact, the choices we make at every stage of life. As we structure our time with choices, it looks as if our lifetime is but a string of choices. That boils down to the reality that we make our life and shape our destiny. " We are not permitted to choose the frame of our destiny. But what we put into it is ours, "says Dag Hammerskjold, the late UN secretary General. Yes, your life is what you make

and your destiny is in your hands. "Life is worth living, we can say, since it is what we make," says American philosopher William James.

What are your questions in life
"The question of life is not, How much time we have? The question is what shall we do with it," says Anna Robertson Brown, an enlightened 19th century American writer, in *What is Worthwhile*—a book that went into 73 printings and stayed in print for 67 years. She says, "Only one life to live! We all want to make most of it. How can we accomplish the most with the energies and powers at our command? What is worthwhile.... We cannot possibly grasp the whole of life. What is vital? What may we possibly let go?"

"The question that faces every man born in this world is not what should be his purpose, which he should set about to achieve, but just what to do with life," says Lin Yutang, a Chinese-American writer. "The answer, that he should order his life so that he can find the greatest happiness in it, is more a practical question, similar to that of how a man should spend his weekend than a metaphysical question as to what is the mystic purpose of his life in the scheme of the universe." Yes, it would be more practical to ask the question: "How can we spend our life joyfully, the way we want?" Perhaps, it is wise to think how best we can live our short life.

Discover the direction and purpose of your life
You have to recognise that there is a certain purpose in life that transcends the fulfilment of material wants. Many people believe that the present social order in which division, falsehood and intolerance prevail has to be replaced by a new order in which humanity, truth and brotherhood reign. This is indeed a laudable ideal goal; but at the individual level each one of us has our own

goals in life. Their purpose and direction are specific to us. Our joy and happiness are prime concerns in life.

Ask yourself what all you would like to do in your short life. What is your life/work direction? What are you planning to achieve. If you are in 20's, it is natural that you have a big appetite for life; you may still be undecided about what you want in life. If you are in 30's you are probably trying to eke out a living or make a successful career; thus laying the foundation for your future. If you are in 40's and 50's, your earnings may have reached peak levels, you are well adjusted with your spouse and your children are being groomed for a better life. If you are in 60's, it is likely that your children are getting settled; and you are planning a retired life. Every time you think you have made the right decision, new priorities keep goading to change direction. So, you redirect your efforts to do something new, something different every time.

You are always looking for new directions, as if you are in search of a new meaning in life. Have you ever thought about it? Everybody gets a lot of chances to look at life and change direction, though nobody gets more than one chance to live. You too can change the direction in life at any stage. Come, rediscover the splendour of a joyful life.

"If you learn to listen, your inner voice will speak to you about your path, your job on earth," says Psychotherapist Tina Tessina. "This wisdom that is directing you from within is your birth right, an inner message, inner voice. You can picture your future. Picture your path. Make some choices. Do research. Allow fantasy time to develop into reality. A wonderful fantasy energises you to bring it into reality. As you learn the requirements of achieving real results, you will find the idea how your future should look gradually maturing and becoming more realistic."

You can reprogramme your mind

We get easily influenced by society's norms for successful life, if not get distracted by others' ideas of good life. Sometimes we can't listen to our inner voice because the cacophony around drowns us in its noise. Because of this reason, sometimes we are not clear about the direction and purpose of life. But never underestimate the powers of your mind. You know intuitively what is good for you in the long run. Listen to the subtle inner voice knocking from within—you will know. Ask a soul searching question: What I really want in my life?

Think of all the things you are missing in life. If joy and happiness are included in that list, then what's the use of the brilliant flashes of genius and the surge of creative ideas that you have. You are here to make use of your mind and body. Use them to reshape your life so that you can enjoy it while you are alive. Redesign a lifestyle that is uncluttered and joyful, focusing on the activities of your interest and the family.

You have a wonderful mind that never stops learning. It can learn what you teach. There are a few basic things to learn to enjoy life:

- *Recognise the fact that your life as a human being is a great blessing.* Your tryst with life is a great blessing. Understand that you are a special being. Appreciate your uniqueness. Realise, how blessed you are.
- *Understand that the gift of life, like any other gift, is meant for your happiness.* Life is a special gift with a condition: you can enjoy it only one term. Nobody gets a second chance. If nature has a purpose in giving life, it surely meant us to live joyfully. Joy of this gift belongs to those who unwrap it. It implies that you should look for happiness in life, and enjoy what you get. It is not wise to expect beyond what life can offer you.

- *Remember, you have the power to live your life, the way you want.* You are the architect of your own life. You have a lot of choices to make. You can define your own destiny. You can live a joyful life.
- *Recall and reminisce joyful moments in life.* You have a natural tendency to remember sweet memories, and forget the unhappy ones. Go ahead, recall joyful memories whenever you want and create your own paradise; surely, that can make your life joyful.
- *Count your blessings.* All the things in life are no less than blessings—blessings and opportunities to learn, to love, to rejoice and to celebrate living, and to share joy with other fellow beings. Think of all the good things in your life; and reminisce all the happy events and relive the joyful moments.
- *Be grateful for good things in your life.*

"Be grateful for yourself," says William Saroyan, American humanitarian writer.

"Yes, for yourself. Be thankful. Understand what a man is, is something he can be grateful for and ought to be grateful for." You must be grateful and thankful for the joy that life offers you.

You can redesign your life: learn to live a joyful life

"They go to heaven and still cry," is an old saying. Yes, we all know that living is a blissful state, no less than a heaven on earth; yet we don't know why we complain. In fact, we have unlimited freedom to live the way we want. It does not mean we should choose to grouse, ignoring all the blessings in life. You have to realise this while you are still alive, because there is nothing you can enjoy once you are dead. Realise this and learn to live a joyful life, of course, on your own terms!

Come discover the joy of living

"To live is to be happy, to be carefree and be overwhelmed by the glory of it all." Not to be happy is living death", says American artist late Everett Ruess. Another great soul Will Durant says, "Drink the brimming cup of life to the full and to the end, and thank God and nature for its challenges, its gifts of beauty, wisdom, labour and love". Come, discover the joy of living!

2

Live Here and Now: Adjust to the Changing World

> The place to be happy is here, time to be happy is now.
> *Robert Ingersol (1833-1899)*
> US attorney, Orator
>
> If you are not happy here and now you never will be.
> *Taisen Desimaru (1914 -1982)*
> Japanese Zen master

The universe is mind blowing

The greatest secret in the entire universe is its origin. Mankind's knowledge about the universe is very limited. Scientists believe that the cosmic evolution began 15 billion years ago. Nobody knows how it came into being nor the extent of the expanding space. We don't know much about the countless galaxies that contain millions of stars. Equally baffling is the distance between them—each a few million light years apart. Each star is indeed a wonder in itself. Take for example, our sun. How wonderful is the solar system, and the meticulous movement of its planets and satellites and their perfect timing. The earth is said to have come into being 46,000 million years ago.

Life on earth is a miraculous exception in the entire universe; and there is no evidence as of now of life anywhere else. Many religions strongly believe that God created all living beings on earth. But the evolutionary scientists believe that, by sheer accident of nature, a single inert molecule jumped into life 3,500 million years ago. How it went on multiplying and evolving into various species is still a mystery that defies explanation. Nobody knows the truth. And the arrival of man—the most intelligent being on earth—is indeed the most surprising development in the entire history of evolution of life on earth.

Human brain is another amazing wonder—a mini-universe in itself with a staggering network of more than a 100 thousand million brain cells called neurons. No one knows how it functions with its marvellous memory. And the existence of the invisible mind that knows, learns, thinks and imagines, is perhaps the greatest mystery. It is your mind that tells about your place in this world. Yes, everything in the universe is mind blowing! While our mind reminds the insignificance of man's existence in the universe, we must recognise the genius of human mind.

The World Is Ever Changing

From Greek philosopher Heraclitus and Buddha to modern scientists, everyone came to realise that everything in the world is undergoing constant change. Another Greek philosopher Anaxagoras says that the world is always in a state of flux. Nothing seems to be everlasting except change! Change is the only constant factor. Time changes anything, almost everything.

Yes, everything around is changing, have you noticed? Look out through the window, you will observe changes everywhere. Nothing remains the same forever. Every human being undergoes change from birth to death — that includes you. You are not an exception. Your whole life can change in a fraction of a second. By the time you finish reading this page your heart *will* have beaten a few hundred times; and it *will* have worn out to some extent. Your brain will have strained a bit; as a result a few neurons will have died. Your lifetime *will* have been reduced by a few minutes. Yes, you are changing every second, but you never know how it is taking place!

It is this alarming state of transition from change to change that compels us to somehow adjust. Those living beings that did not adapt have become extinct. Soon man had realised that adapting to natural changes is the only way for survival. That is why, he always strives to adjust to natural changes to ensure his comfortable living. The secret of resilience of human race lies in its genius for adjustment to the changing environment.

When we see things that we can change, we see them as our problems; and when we cannot change, we accept them as facts of life. By changing things we create real objects out of dreams and fantasies. "The reasonable man adapts himself to the world," says Nobel laureate George Bernard Shaw. " Unreasonable one persists in trying to adapt and change the world to suit his needs. Therefore all progress depends on the unreasonable man." It has been said that changing things is central to leadership; changing them before anyone does is creativity.

All change is not growth, as all movement is not forward. Yet changes can bring surprising progress. Almost every scientific endeavour is in the direction of adaptation to changing nature. In the process, science and technology are progressing at an incredible pace and computing is getting increasingly pervasive. Scientific discoveries and technological inventions are multiplying every year in geometric progression. Advanced technologies, electronic gadgets and hi-tech gizmos are the order of the day.

We have to be aware of the ongoing changes within ourselves and without. If we don't adapt to this changing world we will soon be out of place. Winds of change that sweep the world today call for greater flexibility and faster adaptability. Constant adjustment to the changes in life is one of the secrets of happy living.

Past and Future Are Created by Mind

Human life is indeed a very short voyage in the eternal stream of time. Yet for his convenience, man has divided his lifetime into past, future and present. To him it looks as if this dynamic movement of life is caught between past and future. In reality they do not exist, but nonetheless they appear real to him. He takes it as the universal truth. His mind operates on this premise. As he believes in this kind of axiom his experience follows this belief. It looks as if this kind of thinking is the prime mover of his life. It is almost the sole basis of his actions. All this is because he believes in his mind, which believes in the past, future and the present.

It is natural for man to recall the past or think about future while living in the present. Because of this reason, "The present is saturated with past and pregnant with future," observes German philosopher Leibniz.

When we look into the future our hopes and fears play an important role in our lives. With great hope we entertain fantastic dreams and expect great future. And when we are reminded of the uncertain nature of future we are bogged down by unreasonable fears. But if we can draw inspiration from our dreams and fantasies, and build up realistic future plans we can have wonderful time in the present.

Visit the Memories of Your Past

Memories of our past always remain in our mind. Their most important function is to help us reminisce the good old times in life. Another significant purpose is to help us draw lessons from our unhappy experiences. Let us consider what inspiration can we draw from the past. We must rejoice in our ability to discriminate the pleasant experiences from the unpleasant ones. While the pleasant experiences enhance our joy of living, the unpleasant ones teach us what there is to learn from life.

When we remember pleasant experiences
Each happiness of yesterday is a memory for today and tomorrow. And each pleasant memory makes us happy every time we recall it. Perhaps that is the very purpose it serves.

Relish the sweet memories of your achievements
All of us have lot of achievements to our credit. Yet, we often ponder over the failures unhappily, ignoring the triumphs that are so dear to us. Why not we bring to our mind our successful achievements to make the present moments more enjoyable? Think of the moments of your triumphant glory and all the events of success in your life. Sweet memories always gladden our hearts, as they bring back the moments we cherish. They are a great source of joy in the present. They are associated with satiation of needs and satisfaction of desires, realisation of dreams and achievement of goals. They are also linked with our successes and achievements. Memories of success flatter our ego and delight the heart.

Memories of success will reinforce self-confidence
Sweet memories of successes will build self-confidence, and enhance our self-worth. Acknowledging successes will raise our self-esteem. They will definitely infuse new strengths to our self esteem—that is what makes us proud of ourselves.

Revoke conscience in your actions
The immoral connotations, if any, of our successful achievements act like a policeman with a handbook of traffic regulations. If caught, we may have to pay the fine but the feelings of insult and embarrassment will never fade away. But the redeeming effect is that it stirs our conscience, reminds us of our moral obligations, regulates our behaviour and builds character. Achieving success with a clear conscience will always direct us to do the right things for larger good.

When we remember unpleasant experiences
Like the reheated coffee, recalled unhappy events cause bitterness, says Theresa Chueng in *Coffee Wisdom*. They cause nothing but bitterness and rancour all around. She says, "Regret, guilt, and blame drag you back into the past and do nothing to improve your present situation."

Memories of unpleasant experiences often keep coming up. As our mind continues to dwell on them, it does not appear to be respecting our wish to forget. Have you ever wondered why it does so? It is necessary then to know why your own well wishing life-partner behaves in this fashion. There must be a serious purpose behind. May be it wants you to learn some important lessons in life. Unpleasant experiences may depress you for a while; but if you look at their positive side you can appreciate them. They can teach us what there is to learn in life. Perhaps that is their greatest contribution.

Learn from mistakes and failures
We are born to learn and enjoy life. Don't you remember those childhood joys of learning to ride a bicycle? How many times did we stumble? Remember those small bruises, with smears of blood and that scratch on the knee-cap. It is all part of the excitement and joy of learning. That's how the pleasures of riding began. Soon we enjoyed the motorbike riding; and of course some lucky ones got a sports car. The point here is about the inevitability of setbacks and failures. They are absolutely necessary to help us learn and enjoy. When we try new things, mistakes are bound to happen. But remember, they can help us find the right direction towards success. Our failures cannot undermine us, they can only bolster our determination to achieve!

Be kind to forgive setbacks and failures
Who can be right all the time? We must accept the premise that 'to err is human.' We must always be ready to repair the damage

inflicted by our failures and mistakes upon our self image. Mistakes are very common because nobody is perfect. Don't feel sorry when undesirable things happen without notice; and don't feel guilty for the unintended acts that turned out to be wrong. These thoughts can make us depressed and miserable, if you take them seriously. Therefore it is crucial not to succumb to the feelings of disappointment. One thing is certain, these setbacks and failures can never strike you down. They can only increase your determination to fight back. If they raise their ugly heads, crush them with your *Brahmastra*—memories of your triumphant successes.

The next thing to do is, to forgive yourself for the mistakes you never intended to commit. This will defuse the bitterness of setbacks and failures. Forgiveness is a noble and kind act that mellows the hurt feelings and calms the agitating emotions. It heals your pained heart and eases your strained mind. You must forgive yourself, and rise above these failures to maintain your self-image. Only then can you be humble, free of aggrandisement.

Psychologist Martin E.P. Seligman believes there is an inverse relationship between unforgiveness and satisfaction. He says, "Increasing your gratitude about good things in your past intensifies positive memories, and learning how to forgive past wrongs defuses the bitterness that makes satisfaction impossible".

He suggests two ways of bringing these feelings about past well into the region of contentment and satisfaction. Gratitude exemplifies the savouring and appreciation of good events gone by; and rewriting history by forgiveness loosens the power of bad events to embitter ; and actually transforms bad memories into good ones.

Forget those tormenting thoughts
It is true that we are sometimes troubled by our painful past. The greatest thing we can do is to let go of the unhappy memories,

otherwise they can disturb us if not depress us. It is emotionally draining to indulge in such thoughts. Our feelings are like our servants; and it is not proper for them to rule over their master (you). We must enforce discipline and show them the place where they belong. This is possible if we can wield the armour of joyful memories. It is not worthwhile paying attention to spilt milk when we have plenty to enjoy. If you savour your successes as often as you can, the memories of unhappy thoughts will vanish like the morning mist before the rising sun.

Visit Your Future

Future is uncertain
Our future is always beginning now. Every time we plan to do something we look far beyond. When we think of future everyone of us is anxious—that vague sense of dread and uncertainty about what is going to happen. If we are in control of events happening right now, and if we are able to handle them confidently, we will not be much worried about future. We can get rid of those feelings of insecurity, if we develop self-confidence. Take charge and learn to deal with things, whatever they are; If you do well today, future will take care of itself. Babylonian Talmud (a Jewish Law book) says "Do not worry about tomorrow's troubles, for you do not know what the day may bring. Tomorrow may come but you will be no more, and so you will have worried about a world that is not yours."

Go on a pleasure trip to dreamland

Fly to creative realm: dream what you wish
Come to dreamland. It is a fairy land with dream-like setting, misty and enchanting. It has all the fairy tale elements. The horizon of your fantasies is endless; and sky is the limit for your wishful dreams. Here you can create mesmerising dreams and

exotic fantasies out of your own unfulfilled wishes. This is the place to dream and day-dream what all you wish to do in life. It is here you develop your aspirations and ambitions to achieve what you want in life. You can visualise and enjoy before you realise them.

Visit futuristic domain: make your future plans
In all human endeavours the cause is always there in the future while the effect is right here in the present. We must think of our goals and start working now towards their achievement. Future vision is a must before we do anything important in life. Future plans are necessary before we try to achieve anything in life. But remember the warning of journalist Richard Corliss: "Nothing ages as quickly as yesterday's vision of future."

We cannot rewrite the past but we can look for a secure future. Look beyond the present and search for a proper setting for the future. Keep in mind your abilities and the circumstances, consider the possibilities and opportunities, set realistic goals and work out a plan of action to achieve whatever you want.

Explore the dark zone
The uncertain nature of future induces fear in all of us. Every time we think of unexpected happenings in life we are driven mad to imagine what might be in store for us. "The courage to imagine the otherwise is our greatest resource, adding colour and suspense to all our life," says American Social Historian Daniel J. Boorstin. We start guessing the possible dangers, and various ways we may like to deal with them. It is like groping in the dark in search of a way out. And the fear of the unknown sometimes undermines our self-confidence and our ability to deal with unexpected dangers. Since they are only imaginary dangers, there is nothing to fear. But we must learn to deal with dark new complexities in life when we have to face them in real life. Remember, peace is nothing but freedom from disturbing fear.

Visit the house of horrors
Enjoy the funny scare: "The only thing we have to fear is fear itself—nameless unreasoning, unjustified terror which paralyse needed efforts to convert retreat into advance," says former US President Franklin D Roosevelt. Fears are like paper tigers; they cannot harm us unless we choose to hurt ourselves. They can only scare us, at the most. This is the realisation that helps us enjoy the 'funny scare' in the horror movies. They help us discriminate funny scare from real dangers that can harm us. On the other hand, imaginary horrors can prepare us to deal with real dangers when they happen.

Overcome fear of the future: "Fear is the most paralysing of all emotions. It can stiffen the muscles and stupefy the mind and will", says American author Arthur Gordon (*Reader's Digest*, Aug '87). It is natural for us to be terrified when danger strikes. But when we think of dangers that might happen, we are equally perturbed with anxious thoughts. We have seen horrible things happening in this world; and where is the guarantee that they will not happen to us. This apprehension induces fear and conflict. "They keep the mind in a state of vulnerability that in turn makes the terrain of our life very hard and quite frightening," says counsellor Hugh Prather in *Shining Through*. " There are times we don't even know what we are afraid of. We avoid something we are not even sure is there."

Never forget that the dark side of fear has a flip side as well. If we look at the positive side of your fear you might appreciate it. Professor Michael Pritchard says, "Fear is a little dark room where negatives are developed." Find out how the positives look. Fear compels us to take necessary precautions to save ourselves.

Visit the house of torture: gain endurance and resilience
Haunting nightmares can make us suffer imaginary torture; thank heavens that they are not real. Nevertheless they bring unexpected blessings. It is suffering that develops the powers of the mind—hope, endurance, fortitude, and resilience. Hope will always promise new possibilities for a joyful life. Endurance will give the courage to deal with any frustrating situation in life. Fortitude will see you through all the troubles in the world. And resilience will make you bounce back from sufferings. These blessings will help us deal with sufferings and overcome anything on the way to a happy life.

Never ignore the reality in the present : accept what is

When we don't see reality it seems to be working against our wishes. Sometimes we try to do impossible things or attempt things without the required means. Naturally we end up in a mess. That may be the result of doing things against reality. You must accept the responsibility for ignoring the elements of reality—possibility, feasibility, skills, means, men, money, materials, effort, etc. A failure is perhaps the reality's way of warning when we attempt foolish things. Remember, life is a tight rope walk on reality. All of life is on the wire, all else is watching. If you fall, it makes no difference to anyone except you. Don't ever blame that you are the victim of circumstances, society or people.

So, don't have any illusions about life. Be realistic. Avoiding reality is not the solution. "Emotional sickness is avoiding reality at any cost," says American author M. Scott Peck. "Emotional health is accepting reality at any cost." The sensible thing then, is to make the best use of the way things turn out. An American philosophical thinker Werner Erhard says, "Happiness is a function of accepting what is." Remember, once you accept reality, a great legion of feasible options will be at your command.

Once you accept reality you will be in control of your destiny. You can change things the way you want and manage those you cannot change. This recognition led American theologian Reinhold Niebuhr to come up with the following serenity prayer:

> God, grant me
> The serenity
> To accept things
> That I can not change;
> Grant me the courage
> To change things
> That I can;
> And wisdom
> To know the difference.

Present is the only true reality
Find your place in the real world. "The only true reality is the present," says American author Wayne Amos in *Eternity's Sunrise* (*Reader's Digest*, April 1965). "The past is gone and the future is not yet. It is the present moment that matters." Right now we are living in the present; and we are talking about our life—our real life in the present.

It is quite disturbing to see the present state of the world endangered by fanatic nationalism, uncompromising religious sentiments, meaningless ethnic prejudices, and cut-throat self-centeredness. Besides, there is so much of unwanted information overload—from newspapers, magazines, TV programmes, talk shows and video films—that batters us all the time. And the important matters of family welfare, spouse and children, unfinished work, fleeting health, safety concerns and financial problems keep perturbing us every moment. As our mind sees misery and insecurity at every turn, it drifts into the past seeking escape or looks forward to the future uneasily with a sense of hope. In the process we miss many things in the present; most importantly our personal happiness and joy. This is the tragedy of the unlived life in the present.

A careful examination of our past experiences would certainly offer meaningful insights powerful enough to steer our actions throughout our life. And it is also natural to think about the future course of action before we attempt to do anything. But we must not lose track of the present which is all that is there in life. "Insufficient appreciation and savouring of good events in your past and overemphasis of the bad ones are two culprits that undermine serenity, contentment and satisfaction," says psychologist Martin E P Seligman.

Dag Hammarskjold, the late UN Secretary General exhorts the philosophy of the present-moment-living in the following poem:

For all that has been, thanks
For all that will be, yes
Do not look back.
It will neither give you back the past
Nor will satisfy your other dreams
Your duty, your reward,
Your destiny are here and now.

Nothing is more precious than this living moment. Try to optimise every moment of your life; because these moments ultimately make your life. Try to get the best of your life. Your life is made up of what you make. Then, why not make it the best you can!

Cultivate living in the present: live one day at a time

We are gifted with a human life that is full of blessings. But on one condition : we are permitted to enjoy it for only *one* term. Nobody gets a second chance to savour life again! Remember, *nobody*. Then, why not make it wonderful by committing to enjoy it. Of course, we have a choice: we can either enjoy it or couldn't care less. But if we choose to enjoy our life, we can make it a many splendoured heaven.

So much of our life is spent preparing for distant tomorrows that we often forget that *this* moment will not come again. Why throw it away in daily anxiety about next week or next year? Perhaps we are most alive when consumed by awareness of the present. "Now is the hour—if you're living in the present," says American writer Elizabeth Janeway in "The Time of Your Life" (*Reader's Digest,* April '66). She says, "Weren't the old days better?" we ask ourselves, " Or if not, isn't the future going to be sublime?" Few voices are ever raised to speak for *now.* And yet, no one has ever managed to live in that sublime future or that golden past. *Now* is all we have."

Janeway says, "We must try thinking of time differently. Is its value *really* that it lets us get something done? or is its value simply that that it lets us be, lets us live, lets us *experience?* Time is neutral, neither enemy nor friend, and the passing moment is also the moment that does not pass. When we accept this, when we let ourselves sink into this eternal *now,* something happens. Spare time and work time and busy time all slide together and become one — time for living."

"The only thing we have in this life that really belong to us is what we have lived through. The only way we can take possession of this birthright is by letting our lives happen to us—not passively, but with receptive response, by *being* as well as doing. To be present in this act, to understand, to feel things as they happen—this is what life offers. Be busy or lazy, as you please, but be *there*."

Right now we are living and we are talking about our life—the real life in the present. "Present moment living, getting in touch with your "now" is at the heart of effective living. When you think about it, there is really no other moment you can live.

Live Here and Now: Adjust to the Changing World • 31

Now is all there is and the future is another moment to live when it arrives. One thing is certain, you cannot live it until it arrives," says psychotherapist Wayne Dyer.

Yesterday is gone, tomorrow is not yet in. You have just one day, today. Try to rejoice and be glad in it. "Don't worry about future; it will be here soon enough," assures German philosopher Johaan Wolfgang von Goethe. "Start building it today moment by moment. Nothing is more than this day." Don't anticipate happiness of tomorrow but discover it today. " If you are not happy today, you will never be happy," says American writer Anna Robertson Brown. "Strive to be patient, unselfish, purposeful, strong, eager and work mightily! If you do these things with grateful heart, you will be happy—at least as happy as it is given man to be on earth." American journalist Jean Bell Mosley says, "Concentrate for a moment all that you see, hear, smell, and feel for one exquisite moment. You may sense meaning of life." American author Anne Morrow Lindberg says, "If you surrender completely to the moments as they pass, you live more richly those moments."

People move from place to place most of the time with the assumption that 'everything in life is somewhere else.' If you want to enjoy life, you must get rid of this attitude. You must learn to be happy where you are, before you go elsewhere looking for joy. Yes, now is the time to live in the present and be happy! Seize from every moment its unique novelty, do not postpone enjoying the present moment. "It is the act of staying in the moment that gives immense, immeasurable joy. To me such joy is the ultimate and true measure of success." says Geet Sethi, the seven times World Billiards Champion in *Success vs Joy*. It is his simple formula for joy and success. There is one caveat: " To experience joy, you have to be yourself."

"But today well lived makes, every yesterday a dream of happiness, and every tomorrow a vision of hope," reminds classical Sanskrit poet Kalidasa in *Ritusamhara*.

3

Accept Yourself: Realise Hidden Potential

Self reverence, self-knowledge, self-control.
These three alone lead life to sovereign power.

Lord Alfred Tennyson (1809-92)
English poet-laureate

It is the chiefest point of happiness that a man is willing to be what he is.

Desidarius Erasmus (1469-1536)
Humanist, greatest scholar of northern Renaissance

What All You Have is a Wonderful Self: That Is You in Your Body

Your body is visible to everybody, but you are more than your body. You have an invisible dimension that only you can sense: that is your *self*. It is intangible yet invaluable. You may look small in terms of bodily dimensions, but who knows what giant is hidden inside. You must have heard of Napoleon Bonaparte—a puny figure of 5 feet 2 inches. Imagine the giant in him—his self-confidence—that built an empire! Realise the value of self-esteem and self-confidence for achieving anything in this world.

One self but many names: self-image, self-concept, self-esteem, self-confidence, self-worth

Your self-esteem (call it by any name) is your life-partner you can rely upon. It is like your best friend who is always there within you; ready to come to your rescue whenever you need. It is your self-esteem that ultimately determines your destiny.

"If you do not value who and what you are, you will seek to borrow worth from the outer world, you will look for validation from people whom you believe or know or have more than you," says self-help author Alan H. Cohen, in *Why Your Life Sucks and What You Can Do About It*. "Don't give your power away by making someone or something outside of you more important than what's inside of you."

Your self-concept is created by your mind

It is nature that created our body and mind; whereas it is the mind that constructs the reality of the world for us. " Your mind virtually creates things that nature otherwise cannot," says well-known author Donald L Hamilton in the *Mind of Mankind*. Your *self* is one of those things that nature cannot create. Realise, it is your mind that created your *self*. It's indeed an awesome concept!

We are what our mind makes out to be. We decide who we are. Your self-concept is formed by your mind's perception of your own beliefs, assumptions, values, interests, needs, understanding about yourself and your place in this world. Your self-concept affects your beliefs, perceptions and attitudes. More importantly it influences your actions, performance and ultimately the results, which again add to your self-confidence.

Who are you? Discover yourself

Who are you? You have to find it all by yourself. Self-knowledge is something no one can tell you. " Knowing the world is wisdom; knowing yourself is enlightenment," says Lao-Tzu, a Chinese philosopher. Many of the world's greatest minds have believed that our best energies surface only if we love ourselves and rejoice in our uniqueness. Wise men, over the centuries, have believed that the key to success as a person is self-knowledge.

Whatever it is that you recognise—heart, spirit and imagination, quite free from the outside stimulus. And knowledge of that self is, in a sense, all the actual knowledge you can ever have. " Truth shall make you free, but first it shall make you miserable," says psychotherapist Carl R. Rogers. Whatever it is you have to find the truth about yourself.

Some people look for a guru to guide them know their inner self. It only means they lost confidence in their own personal power. It only means they have surrendered their power to someone outside themselves. It only makes them a slave to the external forces. Remember, no one can know what is within yourself. Self declared gurus may impress you with their gimmicks; but one thing is sure: no one can look into you and tell you what really is inside you.

Only you can look within and find out what you are. If you want to achieve anything in this world, the first thing to do is to discover and bolster your self-image. Spend some time alone, and meet yourself and have an internal dialogue. Examine the unexplainable throbbing that engulfs your inner spirit. Be in touch with your interests, values, aspirations, ambitions, dreams and goals in life. Find what exactly you want in life. Watch the changing pattern of your wants as you grow in age. Remember that success, happiness, and peace are general terms. Unless you specify what really they mean to you , they mean nothing. You have to find out what really you want in life.

Believe and trust yourself
"Believe in yourself!", says motivational speaker Dr Norman Vincent Peale. "Have faith in your abilities! Without humble

but reasonable confidence in your own powers you cannot be successful." Belief in yourself is essential for achieving anything in life. It translates into confidence in your talents and abilities; it manifests itself in the form of pride in whatever you do. Never allow your belief in yourself slip away. "Until you make peace with who you are, you'll never be content with what you have," says American writer Doris Martman. "As soon as you trust yourself you will know how to live," says German philosopher Johann Wolfgang Von Goethe.

Never doubt yourself

Setbacks in life do have several negative effects. Whenever we encounter failures we often doubt our ability to succeed in life. When haunted by self-doubt, self-criticism and self-condemnation, an individual's belief in self may slip away. In fact, there is not a single person on earth without an iota of self-doubt; but the problem arises only when an overdose of it pulls down the individual to the level of an inferior being. A preoccupation with self-doubt is quite agonizing. This kind of negative self-evaluation induces self-pity; and lowers self-esteem. " Self pity is our worst enemy and if we yield to it , we can never do anything wise in the world," says Helen Keller, a born blind, dumb and deaf.

Poor self-image is reflected in below average performance. An individual with low self-esteem often doubts his chances of success. His self-doubt might even sabotage his success. He hesitates to take up responsibilities, fears rejection, does not accept criticism, always looks for encouragement and reinforcement. He may even suffer from lack of social skills, loneliness and depression. For people with insufficient self-confidence life can be an endless struggle. Most unhappy people are so because they live their life in chains of self-doubt and low self-esteem ; they don't even know they have the key. Self-doubts are never easy to resolve. They take time. But there is a lot one can do by focussing on personal strengths and relying on self-esteem.

People with self-doubt invent personal problems for themselves, as if the troubles in the world are not enough. But they don't try to find the solutions. This is what hinders personal progress and happiness. Life is like riding a bicycle. You don't fall off unless you stop peddling. You know who is responsible for that bruise on the knee. If you blame yourself you are creating problems for yourself. On the other hand, if you start blaming people, you are creating problems for others. You must learn to deal with problems rather than creating them. If you don't do that, it will be hard on you; you don't know where you will end up.

Accept yourself

Some men use wigs to cover up their bald heads. Some women dye their white hair to hide their age. They think it gives them a young look. Yes, such cover up actions may give them a temporary relief; but the lurking danger from their feelings of inadequacy continue to bother them. They think that they are doing it to gain acceptance from people around. No matter what you do, some people accept you and others don't. And many people neither notice you nor are bothered about you. At the most it draws attention of some people. They know you are trying to be what you are not; and they pity you for not accepting your age.

The secret of accepting yourself is in loving yourself. A familiar example is a mother's love for her daughter. A mother will always say her daughter is beautiful, even if others disagree. That is because she accepts her daughter, no matter how she looks—beautiful, fair or plain. In the same way you must develop a liking for yourself, without bothering about other's evaluation. If you don't accept yourself, how are you justified in expecting others to accept you?

Recently psychologists at McGill university found that "peoples' feelings of insecurity are largely based on worries about whether they will be liked, accepted and valued by their peers and significant others." But there is no reason to worry, if you listen to the advice of psychiatrist Dr. David Burns: "Perhaps you feel you won't impress others because they are more confident, successful, intelligent and attractive than you are. Such thinking is wrong-headed. The secret of doing well with others is the acceptance of yourself. No matter what you are like–whether you are rich or poor, insecure or outgoing, brilliant or average, attractive or plain—some people will like you and others couldn't care less. *Nobody* gets accepted by everyone. But if you accept yourself, then far more people will accept you." Yes, it does not matter what we do until we accept ourselves. Once we accept ourselves it does not matter what we do.

Keep Up Your Self-esteem
Raise your self-esteem. Be positive always. Never be perturbed by negative things. If any such thing happens, remember that most of the deficit experienced on any occasion will be made up in another. Remember, life will never let you down. You know it. You have seen it happen several times. So, be bullish on life!

Psychologists remind us the need to nurture self-esteem even at the stage of childhood. A child's self-esteem begins from the time he starts asserting to seek independence even to do small things on his own. Over-protection usually lowers a child's self-confidence, as a result he loses his sense of identity and personal strength. Feelings of inadequacy due to low self-esteem reach their peak in adolescent years. Encouragement from parents, positive strokes from teachers, other significant people and peers are crucial for the development of self-esteem. " There are ways to teach a child to appreciate his genuine significance, regardless of the shape of his nose or the size of his ears or efficiency of his mind," says psychologist James Dobson. "Every child is entitled to hold up his head in confidence and security. Self-esteem—that precious sense of personal worth—can provide our child with inner strength to survive the hazards of growing up."

Self-confidence is inside everyone of us. It is like a young man eagerly looking for an opportunity to show what he can do in life. Once we positively tune an individual, the motivation to discover self-confidence comes from within with unexpected force like the fizz in a champagne bottle.

Your values guide your life

Our values are perhaps the deciding factor in life. Our choices in life are influenced by a combination of the values we live by. We were taught that we should shun the seven deadly sins: Pride, Envy, Anger, Sloth, Greed, Gluttony and Lust. Father Alban McCoy, a Catholic chaplain at Cambridge University says," Much about human nature changes, but much remains constant. The seven deadly sins ... are still a valid way of describing the deepest and most corrosive propensities that we share. If anything, they cash out in modern terms pretty easily. They manifest themselves in different ways, but at root they are the same problems."

On the other hand a different view is revealed in a recent survey sponsored by BBC. Ross Kelly, the presenter, reported that the old sins are replaced now by a new set of sins: Cruelty, Adultery, Bigotry, Dishonesty, Hypocrisy, Greed, and Selfishness. He says, "We're less concerned with the seven deadly sins and more concerned with actions that hurt others. For instance we are less bothered about anger than we are about cruelty; and while many of us actually enjoy lust, we still frown on adultery."

All of us have a set of values that guide our behaviour. Psychologists have identified economic values, aesthetic values, scientific values, religious and spiritual values, social and cultural values. People have different profiles of values, with varying degrees of importance. Though many of our values get modified in tune with the changing times, there are certain values in life that are reasonably stable over a period of time. Our core values remain relatively stable.

In "Five Enduring Values for Your Child" (*Reader's Digest*, Dec'81), American author Ardis Whitman says, "Times change. So do our customs—and even moral codes. But certain qualities abide. No matter how times change we will always have the same need our ancestors did to live out our lives in joy and courage, to get along with our fellowmen, and hold on to those values which show us how to grow, to learn and to become better people." She says at least there are five core values that keep us going: joy, love, honesty, courage, faith. We better cultivate these abiding values for joyful living.

Another enlightened soul Anna Robertson Brown suggests ideal values for happy living. American writer Nordi Reeder Campion tells about Brown's views in "What Really Is Worthwhile" (*Reader's Digest*, May '95). "We may let go all things which we cannot carry into eternal life," says Brown. With this yardstick this God-fearing lady measures her values and establishes her rules. She gives a list of things we have to let go:
- Drop pretense
- Drop worry
- Let go of discontent
- Let go of self-seeking

"What are the things in life that we should keep, guard, use?" asks Brown. According to her, eight values can enrich one's life:
- Be wise in the use of time
- Value work
- See happiness each day
- Cherish love
- Keep ambition in check

- Embrace friendship
- Do not fear sorrow
- Cherish faith

Yes, indeed our values guide our lives. Though they keep changing with time, there will be some core values that direct our actions in life and ultimately our destiny.

Discover your hidden potential

You must realise that you have something special in you, something admirably unique, because every person is designed to be unique. You must unearth your hidden wealth— your creative gifts, your talents, your special abilities, so that you can do anything in this world. These things can be actualised during your lifetime. Once you discover what they are, you will probably like yourself. If you can appreciate that uniqueness, you will soon love yourself and accept every aspect of yourself.

You will stand in awe, once you know your potential. Just imagine the potential of a 100 thousand million brain cells in your head. You are almost limitless in your capabilities. Yes, the only limitations we have are those we put on ourselves. The genius of man is always beyond reason and imagination; and the might of human intellect is boundless. "It is evident that our organism has stored-up several reserves of energy that are ordinarily not called upon—deeper and deeper strata of explosible material, ready for use by any one who probes so deep," says American philosopher William James in *Your Secret Strength* (*Reader's Digest*, April '75). " The human individual usually lives far within his limits. In rough terms , we may say that a man who energises below his normal maximum fails by just so much to profit by his chance at life."

"The life of ours has been filled with gifts of the divine giver," reminds Nobel-laureate Rabindranath Tagore. Behind every natural gift you are given, there is a wish for your happiness. But one thing is certain, if you don't unwrap them you can't enjoy them.

Abraham Maslow, a well-known psychologist, believes that there is a tendency in all of us towards 'self-actualisation'. He refers to "capacities clamouring to be used," a restlessness for self development, accomplishment and esteem. One's full potential emerges not by adding skills but first unlocking the door to internal resources waiting to be tapped. He emphasised the need to bring out the inner potential in every one of us.

"The persons born with a talent they are meant to use will find their greatest happiness in using it," says German philosopher Johann Wolfgang Von Goethe. According to professor John W Gardner of Stanford University, "True happiness involves full use of one's powers and talents." Maxwell Maltz, the psycho-cybernetics guru, says, "One's joy comes, not from fame, but from the joy of exercising one's creative powers." In *Authentic Happiness*, psychologist Martin E P Seligman of the University of Pennsylvania makes an appeal to everybody: "Realise your potential abilities for lasting fulfillment. They are the source of enduring happiness." Yes, all of us can attain greatest success and happiness possible in this life if we use our native capacities to their greatest extent.

"The happiness that is genuinely satisfying is accomplished by the fullest exercise of our faculties and the fullest realisation of the world in which we live," says British philosopher Bertrand Russell. Discover your treasure trove and find the hidden potential. It is like a bunch of raw diamonds; you need to polish them to see how brilliant they are. It is the exhilaration of testing your limits that gives joy; while your achievements make you happy. Happiness also comes from contributing to the happiness of fellow beings in this world.

Be yourself with discipline

"We are responsible for what we are, and whatever we wish ourselves to be, we have the power to make ourselves," says Swami Vivekananda. " If what we are now is the result of our own past actions, it follows that whatever we wish to be in future can be produced by present actions. So, we have to know how to act. This world is a gymnasium where we come to make ourselves to be strong."

Whatever we do we must do it with discipline. It is the difference between what we can do and what we should do. Self-discipline is indeed a mighty weapon. It has been the tool with which many have forged success in life. "Self-discipline is the golden key, without it you cannot be happy," says Maxwell Maltz, the psycho-cybernetics guru.

"To be yourself in a world that is constantly trying to make you something else is the greatest accomplishment," says American writer Ralph Waldo Emerson. Be true to yourself. The trick is not to trick. Like yourself and let others like what really you are. Concentrate on what is worth *being* rather than what is worth having. "When what we are is what we want to be, that's happiness," says Millionaire Malcolm Forbes.

Authenticity makes each person's life count by restoring *power* to the individual. Consider the lives of authentic people like Socrates, St. Francis of Assissi and Mahatma Gandhi. They have the power of example, the power of self-love and the power of spirit. The authentic people have a *sense of direction;* they recognise the direction in which their lives are meant to go. They have *self-generated energy.*

In "The Awesome Power to be Ourselves" (*Reader's Digest,* July '83), American writer Ardis Whitman says, "To be oneself is a natural, human and universal power. Striving for authenticity is not easy. It's a life time endeavour, nobody ever makes it all the way. It is becoming rather than an ending, something we learn day-by-day." She gives some ways to begin:

- *Pay attention to what is going on in your life, inwardly and outwardly.*
  See how you change over time, and see what muffled longings are being expressed.
  Admit your inner conflicts, and listen to the dialogue within. Record them in your diary.
- *Accept the idea that nothing is wrong with being different from other people.*
  The truth is, all of us are different, we are meant to be, whatever we want to be.
  "Each one of us, is a unique being confronting the rest of the world in a unique fashion," says philosopher Paul Weiss. Seek out your deepest convictions and stand by them, live by them.
- *Spend time with yourself*
  Solitude is at the heart of self-knowledge, because when we are alone that we learn to distinguish between the false and the true, the trivial and the important. "As with splitting of the atom, the opening of self gives access to a hidden power," says Whitman. "Authenticity is sensitising and blessed power. It comes with a feeling at home with oneself, and therefore at home in the universe. It is the greatest power in the world—the power to be ourselves".

You can transform your personality: recreate and redefine

You must be wondering how to become the person you always wanted to be. American journalist Ponchitta Pierce explains in "Three Steps to Self-confidence" (*Reader's Digest,* August '76), Speech consultant Dorothy Sarnoff's approach to help the uncertain to 'redesign' their personalities. She says that every person has positive traits. One must "take those strong qualities and put them into the person whose future is at stake—you." In Speech Dynamics course she helps people to be more confident. "It's taking the best of yourself, and making it better."

She observes that people are generally encouraged to look better; but "what good is that when they open their mouths?" She aims "at making people more appealing to both the ear and the eye." She helped people how to look better with appropriate dress; and more importantly, how to impress people with their speech. According to Sarnoff there are three basic keys to redesigning one's personality :

Evaluate yourself
You must be as conscious about your positive side as you are about the negative. Look deep inside yourself and find things you like. Are you imaginative, innovative, compassionate, patient? Acknowledging your good points raises your self-esteem right away. If you find that you have some irritating traits write them down as a first step towards eliminating them. Awareness is the first step in correcting oneself.

To know how others see you, place a mirror near your telephone. How do you look when you speak? Are your eyes alive? Are you sending out negative signals? If so, change them.

Make yourself interesting
When you speak, your voice is important. Wispy voice indicates lack of self-confidence. Listen to your voice on a tape recorder. Is it nasal, high, nagging, apathetic, shrill, whining? Do you speak chop-stock phrases? The body is 'sound sensitive' and such unappealing verbal mannerisms can turn a listener off. Smooth and mellow tone can add warmth to your personality.

One way to make yourself interesting is to take in enough 'food' for conversation to be well informed on many subjects. Skim through current magazines and newspapers, listen to the latest news. Visit museums, attend plays, cultural activities. Use more imagination, a larger vocabulary, more colourful descriptions. Learn to communicate your feelings. If you are shy, learn to ask a 'stimulating question'. Be a good listener and know when to respond.

Be pleasantly assertive
If you want to say 'no,' say it without annoying people. Keep your voice warm and firm and the face smiling. Learn to resist peer pressure by saying no gracefully. Being pleasantly assertive also means knowing how to criticise without tearing down. Begin by acknowledging a few good points saying, "That's a good idea. But do you think you must go at it this way? In this "inverse approach," your ideas come across as constructive suggestions, not as slap-downs.

Don't forget your posture. "Sitting tall and erect, or standing straight helps you look more confident and alert in a conversation." Whether you're asking your boss for a raise, or making a speech, or just talking to friends, 'psych' yourself up constantly. The minute you enter a room with such a mission, say to yourself "I care I know I am coming across well." If you tell yourself often enough you'll soon have solid reason to believe it.

Check what you want: elegance, flair, grace, panache, poise, refinement, sophistication, style. You can develop whatever you want. Your pleasing visual image and good grooming can work wonders for your self-image, raising your self-confidence and self-worth. You can have invincible self-confidence. Once you achieve it, you will know how well you are received in the society. It is not impossible to achieve. The only requirement is your willingness to work with yourself. Be a joyful looking person, soon you will become one!

Recognise you are always growing and becoming

"I am still a work in progress," says Candice Bergen, a Hollywood actress. How profound is her statement! It implies that everyone of us is changing every moment; and like everything in this world, we are changing, growing and becoming. Personal growth and maturity come along with change. "I am happy because I am growing daily; and I am honestly not knowing, where the limit lies," says well-known Karate Master Bruce Lee.

Nobel Laureate Pearl S Buck says, "Growth itself contains the germ of happiness." British Poet WB Yeats says, "Happiness is neither virtue nor pleasure, neither this nor that, but simply growth. We are happy when we are growing." Do you want my one word secret of happiness—it's *growth*, in all aspects of life.

Keep up your character, dignity, honour, and self-respect

We must learn to forgive ourselves, and rise above these failures to maintain our self-respect, which is the basis of our respect for others. Only then it can have true value, can it be humble, free of aggrandisement.

A person devoid of character is not worth a penny. Positive values will add dignity and honour to your character. "One's dignity may be assaulted and cruelly mocked, but cannot be taken away unless it is surrendered," says Hollywood actor Michael J Fox. "What is left when honour is lost," says Greek philosopher Pubilius Cyrus.

"We have put too much stress in recent times on intellect, too little on character," says Pulitzer Prize winning writer Will Durant, "We have sharpened our wits and weakened our restraints." (*Reader's Digest*, March '69). "Character is power: it makes friends, draws patronage and support and opens the way to wealth, honour and happiness," says Canadian artist John Howe. Degrees of happiness vary according to the degrees of virtue, and consequently the life which is most virtuous is most happy.

"Watch your thoughts, they become your words; watch your words, they become your actions; watch your actions, they become your habits; watch your habits, they become your character, watch your character, it becomes your destiny," says American author Frank Outlaw.

Before we close this chapter, it is important to listen to the eternal words of English Poet laureate Lord Alfred Tennyson, once again: "Self reverence, self-knowledge, self-control. These three alone lead life to sovereign power".

4

Take Care of Your Body: That Is Where You Live

A sound mind in a sound body is a short but full description of a happy state in this world.

John Locke (1632-1704)
British Philosopher

The winners in life treat their body as if it were a magnificent spacecraft that gives them the finest transportation and endurance for their lives.

Denis Waitley
American Personal Success Guru

You Are Unique by Design: You Are Special!

Life is a whim of several billion cells to be a human being for a while. Every person is unique by design. Your body is specially made for you; it is so unique that it gives an identity of your own. Your face and limbs are distinct, you don't resemble anybody. Neither your fingerprints nor retinal images match with those of any person living or dead. You are special in many ways—physical and spiritual. You are so different from others that there is no single person like you among the 6.2 billion people living on earth today or among the 30 billion people who had lived before in this world! You are only one of a kind, a class apart. The truth is, incredible as it may seem, there is not a single human being like you in the entire universe. That is a reason good enough to call for a celebration!

Your Brain is the Greatest Marvel in the World

Scientists estimate that the number of cells in human brain at the time of birth is (hold your breath) more than a hundred thousand million (count the zeroes—100,000,000,000). If each cell switches on a light, imagine the brilliance of so many lights! If their job is to light up your life, imagine how bright can be your life path. Go ahead. Switch on as many lights as you can!

Our brain is composed of 3D neural pathways interconnected by synapses. According to the British psychologist Tony Buzan, an authority on memory, the number of permutations and combinations of our brain cells is so staggering that our life time is not enough to count them. When you start thinking about anything, your mind goes on checking all the brain cells to connect the related information. It finishes the job in a fraction of a second. Just imagine the speed of your thought. It is indeed mind blowing!

Its powers of memory are really fantastic. There is room inside the brain for storing every kind of information that demands your attention. Let me tell you about the experiments of a Canadian neurologist Dr. Wilber Penfield. When he tickled the brain of an old lady with a mild electronic probe, she remembered her long forgotten school teacher; and recited a few nursery rhymes. Another woman heard Christmas carols in a church in Holland she attended as a child. Still another relived the birth of her child 20 years before. If a few cells could store so much information, imagine how great is the storing capacity of human brain. It is like an old attic containing the memories of a life time. It can bring back your memories whenever you want.

Neuroscientists tell us that processing stored information by our brain forms the basis for all our intellectual activities. It is an important step in establishing the hierarchy between information, knowledge and wisdom. It is through collation that we convert information into knowledge and subsequently, as we gather further experience, knowledge into wisdom.

The invisible genie in your brain is your mind. It gives 'wisdom' which according to Sophocles " is the supreme part of happiness." Its powers of learning are marvellous. It helps us develop reasoning, problem-solving abilities, creative talents and language skills. Your brain is more powerful than you think it is. It all depends on how well you train your mind and keep it active. Your mind does many things for you:

It gives awareness of your existence.
Helps you to know, learn, think, reason and judge.
Memorises, stores and retrieves information
Gives conscience that helps you know good and bad
Has hidden potential and energies.
Helps you to satisfy your needs
Helps evaluate and discriminate things.
Helps you to solve problems
Helps you to realise dreams and achieve goals.
Helps you to achieve anything.
Helps you to enjoy life and be happy.
Gives you identity, because your mind is you.

You Are Responsible for Your Body
You are now living in your body. It is the only place you have to live in this world. It defines your uniqueness in this world. Everyone recognises your body because it gives you an identity of your own. "Your body is precious. It is our vehicle for awakening," says Gautam Buddha, "Treat it with care."

Like any other living thing your body is subject to time. It undergoes a cycle of growth to decline from birth to death. 'Ageless body' is a myth; no one can make it immortal. What all you can do is keep it hale and healthy as long as you live. "*Jeevan bhadrani pasyate*—ensure you are safe and alive," writes ancient Indian sage

Vyasa in *Mahabharatha*. It implies that you must ensure that you are alive first, for you can't enjoy life if you are dead. Soon there will be a time when plenty of things are available, but you are not there. If you are alive, you know, you can enjoy all the wonderful things in the world.

Breathe fresh life every time: it is vital for survival

Life on earth is indeed a many-splendoured thing. If you want to take a breathtaking view of life there is nothing like breathing exercises. In fact, you are infusing new life every time you breathe, (you know what happens when you don't breathe!).

We often use the phrase "he breathed his last," when someone is dead. This is because breathing is vital for sustaining life. Without breathing life cannot exist. It has been said that a man can live about forty days without food, about three days without water, and about eight minutes without air. It is absolutely true. But the problem is, "unlike most nutrients, oxygen cannot be stored by the body," says American writer Philip Smith, in "Breathe Your Troubles Away" (*Reader's Digest*, Feb.'82). "Every minute we require a steady, fresh intake of air. Yet most of us use our lungs at only one-third of our full capacity." In "Breathe Right and Stay Well" (*Reader's Digest*, April '66), American writer John Frazier quotes William Knowles, another authority on breathing: "Gases fill lung spaces and cheat your tissues of oxygen. Lungs will hold 6 pints of air, yet an office worker inhales only about a pint. This means that five–sixths of your lung capacity lies idle." Your lung dimensions may differ, but the fact remains that there is a great amount of unutilised capacity.

We can increase the intake of oxygen, though we cannot raise the quantum of oxygen in the nature. This can be achieved if we can enlarge the capacity of lungs. The larger the capacity, greater the supply of oxygen for the body. Breathing exercises can greatly improve the capacity of our lungs and facilitate adequate supply of oxygen required by the body. This in turn can improve our health to a great extent with the promise of longevity. We must learn to breathe more, because life-giving oxygen is vital for our survival.

The word *prana* in Sanskrit is the equivalent of the English word 'life'; and *pranayama* means "life giving breathing exercises." In these exercises we virtually inhale life-sustaining vital energy and exhale the harmful toxins. No matter what, we have to keep breathing all through our life to stay alive. But if you want to rev up life in the body, you need plenty of oxygen fuel. Breathing exercises can help you. To keep oneself fit, " It is not necessary to work out in a gymnasium for hours, jog great distances or pedal stationary bicycle for hours on end," says Fitness Expert Jane Brody. "All it takes is 20 to 30 minutes a day of heavy breathing while limbs move rhythmically through air or water," (*Reader's Digest*, Jan.' 91). These exercises can increase longevity, because they actually renew, revitalise and rejuvenate the body. " Whine less, breathe more," says a Swedish proverb.

Keep Yourself Fit and Active: Exercise Regularly

What *is* fitness? Fitness Expert Jane Brody says, " In most simple terms, it is the ability of the body to operate at the optimal capacity for as many years as you live," (*Reader's Digest*, Jan. '91). According to cardiologist Dr. George Sheehan, "Fitness is simply, the ability to do work" (*Reader's Digest*, Nov. '86). "It is movement and energy, not only muscular but also cognitive. I could quote doctors who have found that fitness does lower life-threatening risk factors, or psychologists who argue that it reduces hostility, tension, anxiety. The truth is it does all these wonderful things, but it does more." Here are his simple rules for fitness:
- Eat a nutritious breakfast
- Don't eat between meals
- Maintain your weight

- Don't smoke
- Get a good night's sleep
- Exercise sensibly and regularly

You must have your daily dose of sweating out, and give the exercise your body requires. Otherwise it may become stiff with weak muscles and the body toxins may shorten your life. Exercise is what your muscles instinctively want to do under stress—run or fight. The kinds and amount of exercise needed to reap health benefits are well within the reach of most people: brisk walking, jogging, running in place, cycling, skipping, dancing, swimming, and stair-climbing. If these are not possible for any reason, walk around the block to throw off the bodily tension. Remember, exercise should always be a pleasurable activity. As German scholar Alexander van Humboldt says, "True enjoyment comes from the activity of the mind and exercise of the body : when the two are united."

Health benefits of exercise have been recognised for centuries. As early as 600 BC, an Indian physician used exercises to treat diabetes. Scientists have found several benefits of exercise:

- Makes the heart more efficient; improves blood circulation
- Reduces cholesterol levels
- Reduces the risk of coronary heart disease
- Increases the body's sensitivity to insulin
- Increases the mineral content of bones; prevents osteoporosis
- Reduces the risk of cancer of breast and reproductive systems
- Reduces the loss of lean muscle tissue
- Invigorates the nervous system
- Helps the body weight under control

Listen to body signals and relax

Overwork can damage your body; frequent worries can cause headaches if not depression. Some people prefer to go on a vacation to forget their problems. Everybody says 'relax', but no body tells how. Here again you don't need a guru to tell you when you should relax and how. The most reliable guide is the subtle warnings of your own body. Just as the seismic signals forewarn the impending earthquake, your body signals usually sound the alarm about the possible danger. Any derailed body can tell the story of missed signals!

Sometimes you may feel burned up, overworked, tense, tired, restless, suffer from headaches, heart burns, go short of breath, etc. If you can read these signals you will know in advance when you have to take care of your body to prevent possible collapse. That is the time you need to unwind and take a break and allow the body to recuperate and regain its original shape and strength. "If you listen to the body, 99 per cent of your problems will disappear, and the remaining one per cent will be just accidents, not really problems," says philosopher Osho in *Body Mind Balancing*.

Bodily signals typically announce themselves slowly. The process is insidious and incremental. They often show up as physical symptoms and feelings. Loss of appetite usually associated with weight loss, disturbed sleep, not refreshed by sleep, feel strained and stressed, tired or irritated. If you ignore these signals, they might as well lead to a depressive streak that adds some more harmful symptoms—loss of interest in life, inability to enjoy anything, decreased sexual energy (loss of libido), feelings of loneliness, worthlessness and hopelessness, feelings of guilt and shame, even thoughts of self harm and suicidal tendencies. First requirement to prevent them is your ability to sense the body signals and do what you can before any harm is done.

One purpose of relaxing is to rejuvenate the body and refresh the mind; but the main purpose is to enliven the spirits by enjoying the time. To feel relaxed, just do anything— even nothing! "Even to achieve this non-doing one has to do much," says philosopher Osho in *Meditation: The Art of Ecstasy*. The best thing to do is to sleep whenever you feel tired. Nothing refreshes like a deep sleep. If not, you can as well lie down. But never entertain negative thoughts—they spoil your sober mood. This is perhaps the right time to reminisce joyful moments. If you want to light up your life and buoy up the spirits, recall the sweet memories of pleasant experiences. Think of somebody or something that cheers and relaxes.

If you so like, you may even indulge in joyful activities—hobbies, games, hand work, painting, or whatever, at a leisurely pace without straining yourself. These golden moments of delight will help you to have a good time, and in the process allow you to relax. The whole purpose is to fill your time with joyful moments. Only then, you can rebuild the body to regain its original strength. Once relaxed, look at that sparkle in your eyes and that new spring in your stride! See how refreshed you look, ready to jump into action as usual. After all, the very purpose in life is to enjoy it!

Well-being through diet

"Our bodies are what we eat, plus what our ancestors ate," says social philosopher Will Durant. " Don't let restaurants lure you ; they will burden your flesh in proportion as they lighten your purse. Perhaps one of the cardinal errors of our time and land is that we continue in a sedentary life with the diet that served to provide muscle and heat. The hospitals are littered with people who have allowed an excess of imports over exports to disturb their internal economy."

A recent study by the British scientists indicated that there are health advantages in regularity in food intake over chaotic consumption. 'Eat less and often' seems to be their advice. "For those wishing to optimise their well-being through dietary means, consistency is the order of the day," writes British physician Dr John Briffa. He believes that this pattern of eating will help improve health. Dr. Eugenio Selman-Housein, personal physician to President Fidel Castro, and president of '120 years club' in Havana, believes that "we can extend longevity through healthier diets, moderate exercise and plenty of motivation." If you want to stay alive a little longer, it is absolutely necessary to create conditions for sustaining life in your body. May be you should do something about it.

Don't rush : live at your own pace

People who display Type A behaviour are generally hurried, impatient and easily angered. They do not realise how counterproductive is such behaviour. It is personally and socially undesirable. Doctors say that people with Type A behaviour are sitting ducks for a heart attack. A more contemplative Type B personality is personally beneficial. To ensure longevity of life, everybody needs to develop a relaxed type of personality. Instead of rushing life, you have to allow your life to move at its natural pace. Fitness Expert Jane Brody gives some helpful tips in *"Become a 'Type B,' (Reader's Digest,* Feb. '82):

Assess yourself

- Take stock of your life's goals, how you spend your time, what is really important to you and your loved ones. Concentrate on what is worth *being* rather than what is worth *having*.
- Stop measuring your life in quantities—number of clients, number of committees on which you serve, number of accomplishments. Think more in terms of quality. Rid yourself of trivial obligations. You will probably find doing a few things really well is more ego enhancing than doing a lot less effectively.

- Give up trying to be a super person who despite a demanding career, insists on retaining control of everything at home, entertaining lavishly, participating in community affairs, raising perfect children. This can be done at the expense of your health, your marriage and your children. Forget perfection. At home and at work, decide what it is that you and you alone must do, and delegate the other responsibilities.
- Spend time alone with yourself. Attend a concert, visit a museum, read a thought-provoking book. Listen to music. Or sit quietly and contemplate the sky. Your body appreciates calmness much more than extra sleep.

Slow down
- Did you ever get a feeling that you are going too fast, that you cannot slow down? Work excessively, exercise rigorously, feel like a power station? Dashing to achieve things? Can't concentrate because of great rush of ideas? Can't hold a thought? Think where you are heading? Where you will end up? Well, it is high time you slowed down.
- Leave yourself more time than you think you will need to get somewhere or accomplish something. Then, if you are delayed, you'll have less reason to become anxious.
- Take some thing to read whenever you might have to wait around or stand in line. Or practise doing nothing. Study the people around you. Fantasise. Think about someone you love. Think about your life. Have a pleasant conversation.
- Do not clutter up your calendar with appointments, or create unnecessary deadlines by making appointments for a narrowly specific time. Say "I will be there between 11 and 11.30" rather than " precisely at 11."
- Get up 15 minutes earlier in the morning so you won't have to start your day in a rush. Your body will appreciate the calm much more than extra sleep.

- Stop interrupting others or finishing their sentences. Practise being a good listener, concentrating on what is being said instead of thinking of something that is of great interest to you. And don't take over from someone who is doing a job slowly, unless he cannot do it at all. Walk away if you can't stand to watch.
- Even when working against a deadline, take breaks periodically to chat with a neighbour, stare out of the window, take a walk—anything that will help you to relieve the tension.
- It is not good for you to be always dashing and pushing to achieve things in life. It is better to slow down and do things at your own pace rather than competing with the crowd.

Ease up
- Don't waste your anger on trivial matters, such as a delayed train, an inept waiter, or an abrupt salesman. In most cases you can't do anything about it any way.
- Avoid contact with people who always raise your heckles. Don't take so seriously those you must continue to see. And stop focussing on how many people fall short of your ideals. This will only foster disappointment in and hostility towards others.
- Make friends with a Type B person . He or she may not say much but will listen well and serve as a model of the relaxed behaviour you seek in yourself.

Finally, remember that habitual rushing and excessive competitive hostility are the two forms of behaviour most closely associated with heart attack. Think about what situations annoy you, and call upon your intellect and sense of humour to get you through.

Harness your anger and stress

Anger is an interpersonal phenomenon. It is generally caused by unanswered demands and unmet expectations. It releases tremendous amount of hidden energies to deal with the threatening situation. These energies are generally targeted against the threatening objects. If they are lifeless things they get damaged or destroyed. If it is directed at threatening persons it leads to interpersonal problems. "Anger must be the energy that has not found its right channel," says psychologist Florida Scott-Maxwell. Yes, if we can channel these energies to some other achievable goals, the result would be wonderful.

"Stress is the spice of life," says the Canadian endocrinologist Hans Selye. We all need a pinch of it to spice up our body before we launch into action. Journalist Michele Hanson makes a distinction between 'nice stress' as opposed to the 'nasty stress' we all know. She says, " Nice stress probably includes ruling the world, earning a fortune, having a tight schedule, knowing what you are doing every minute of the day, having a purpose, and knowing where and what you are. This buzzy-type of stress is produced by a hormone called DHEA-S (dehydroepiandro-sterone-S). This leads to better brain and memory function, strengthens body defences, boosts immune system, improves complexion, and lengthens your life." This is the kind of stress we all need to meet the challenging situations in life.

At the same time we should be aware that rushing things in a hurry induces nasty stress that disturbs the normal functioning of the body. Imaginary fears and threats are the main culprits that cause nasty stress. Since the days of dinosaurs, human brain is programmed to respond to frightening situations in one of the three ways: *fight*—to fight back and attack the aggressor or *flight*—to run away from danger or *fright*—to become immobilised with fear. The danger signals trigger other hormones that prepare us to deal with the threats. Heart rate increases, blood pressure shoots up, breathing increases, sweat oozes out, muscles become tense, entire body is under stress. Until the fears are contained the body is overwhelmed by stressful reactions.

Control of fear seems to be the best solution. In *The Conquest of Fear* Basil King gives the best possible advise: *Be bold—and mighty forces will come to your aid.* "Boldness means a deliberate decision, from time to time, to bite off more than you can chew," says American author Arthur Gordon *(Reader's Digest,* Aug.'87). "And there is nothing mysterious about the mighty forces referred to. They are the latent powers that all of us possess: energy, skill, sound judgement, creative ideas—yes, even physical strength and endurance in far greater measure than most of us realise."

Dr. Hans Selye, a Canadian endocrinologist, gives a recipe for the best antidote to the stresses of life: " The first ingredient is to decide whether you are a race horse or a turtle. The second is to choose your goals and make sure that they are really your own, not something imposed on you by others. And the third ingredient to this recipe is altruistic egotism—looking out for yourself by being necessary to others."

Enjoy good health
" Life is not living, but living in health," says Roman poet Martial. " Happiness lies, first of all, in health," says US orator George William Curtis. According to American Transcendentalist Philosopher Ralph Waldo Emerson, " The first wealth is health." He says, " Give me health and a day, I will make the pomp of emperors ridiculous." American Personal Development Expert Denis Waitley says, " Time and health are two precious assets that we don't recognise and appreciate until they have been depleted." So much appeal, in favour of good health that we all enjoy.

At the end, listen to the wise words of philosopher Kahlil Gibran, "Your body is the harp of your soul. And it is yours to bring forth sweet music from it or confused sounds." The choice is yours!

5

Share Life: Enjoy Warm Relationships

To have joy one must share it; happiness was born a twin.
Lord (George Gordon) Byron (1788-1824)
English Romantic Poet, Satirist

Happiness quite unshared, can scarcely be called happiness, it has no taste.
Charlotte Bronte (1816-1855)
English Novelist

The desire to be associated with other human beings is in itself an innate nature of man . Even non-living things like atoms get associated with other atoms. Association is one of the basic properties of things in nature. Association of living beings with non-living things is also very common. It takes the form of attachment, possession, ownership, control. Among the human beings, it takes different forms—love, trust, caring, sharing, welfare, service, influence, control and leadership.

Relationships are for sharing life

Relationships are the web of human life. We all build emotional bridges to establish kinship in this world, because we can't do without other people. Our life depends on the kind of relationships we establish—at our home, school, college, office, business, and every activity in our society. Consider the common scenes of personal encounters—parents kissing and hugging children, children playing, youth holding hands; men and women negotiating for things they want. We often watch young people frantically trying to contact their friends or sms someone over the mobile (often unmindful of the traffic on the road.) We attend all sorts of parties to relate with people. We celebrate the marriage of our children or birth of a child . We see just-married girls and their parents bidding farewell to each other. We visit friends and relatives in hospital or attend condolence meetings. The undertone in all these scenes is the ubiquitous human relationships. Relationships seem to fill our lifetime.

Good network of relationships with people are very important. They are essential for our happiness and comfortable living on this planet. That is the reason why we are ready to give our all to form satisfying relationships with significant people in our lives. Timothy Sharp and his colleagues at The Happiness Institute, Sydney, believe that "only 10 per cent of happiness comes from income and assets; nearly 90 per cent comes from attitude, life control and relationships. So, you don't need millions to be happy; your warm relationships can do the trick!

Our circle of relationships

We form our own circle of relationships depending on our affinity and intensity of relationships. These are the networks that connect with other people. These are the bridges we build to reach out to the society at large. Relationships are essential in our interdependent world.

Close circle

Our close circle of relationships consists of our family members and very close friends whom we love, trust and depend upon. Family members include parents, spouse and children. We can regard members of this group as a loving, caring, sharing, helping and growing group. Sharing warm relationships will confer many mutual benefits on almost all the members of this group.

Second circle
This includes some members of the family, relatives and friends whom we like, but do not know well enough to trust completely or who have some characteristics that make being closer impossible. It also comprises of people we like a lot but who are far away or who cannot be trusted to keep commitments or to respond when we need them.

Third circle
It includes casual friends and acquaintances with whom we have friendly relations. These are the people we know but don't know well enough to consider them as warm friends. For example, friends of our friends, or family members and other people we like and enjoy spending time with; but with whom we have not yet made an individual connection. Some of these people may very well move into our second circle after some time and experience while others may drift away.

Last circle
These are not much closer in our personal life: Circumstantial friends, neighbours, co-workers, people we know at the school or gym or market place or government offices. They are not much closer in our personal life, though some may move into our inner circle later.

How you respond is important in your relationships
Our relationships with people can be explained in terms of stimuli and responses of individuals. "Between stimulus and response man has the freedom to choose," says Austrian psychiatrist Dr. Viktor E Frankl. He notes that with the freedom to choose are those endowments that make us uniquely human. We have self-awareness; imagination to create beyond reality, conscience to see right and wrong, and independent will and ability to act, based on self-awareness. We have the initiative and responsibility to make things happen.

"In our relationships most of the reactions are responses," says American psychotherapist Tina Tessina in *It ends with you*. "That is, you do something (stimulus) and I respond to what you do (response). You respond to my response, and you respond to my counter-response, and so on. There are few original actions or statements.

"This means, if you control your actions and responses, you control a lot of your relationships. Anyone who is willing to do the work necessary to control emotions, reactions, and responses can control a vast majority of relationships. We often don't realise how much our reactions contribute to a partner's behaviour.

"If you take care to speak to your partner and your family in positive, loving ways and address them directly with kindness, you will find that very soon they will begin to be more kind and considerate of you. However, if you yell and nag at your children to 'be nice', they are more likely to yell, or be resentful and sullen, than to be considerate.

"To respond thoughtfully and carefully rather than quickly and automatically is hard. However, mastering self-control, no matter how difficult, is always worthwhile, because it makes every moment of your life easier.

"Self control begins with self awareness. If you already *know* what pushes your buttons, you will be less reactive to it. If you can tell when you are stressed, you can be more cautious at these times.

"You have little control over what people choose to send toward you and total control over what you choose to send out. The control you *do* have over what people send into your world consists in how you *receive* it and respond to it.

"As long as you remember that your responses will go a long way toward shaping the whole interaction, and eventually your whole relationship, and you take the time to control the way you respond, you will see all relationships improve dramatically."

Relationships for learning

"To approach your relationships as a course in personal growth, begin by re-evaluating the purpose of your relationships with significant people in your life," advises psychotherapist Tessina. "Use them as a training ground for learning. Assume that there is a lot to learn from problems, which increase in complexity as you gain knowledge to solve. 'A problem does not exist without a valuable lesson attached.' Never, ever do the problems indicate that you deserve punishment, or you did something bad.

"Just as in school, if you do not understand the lesson and solve the problem you will keep getting it back in altered terms, until you do understand. This is NOT to give you hard time, but to teach you what you need to know to live a fuller, more loving life."

Ten commandments of human relations

We often meet friends and relatives to enjoy their company. Since the fun we get is mutual we always look forward to renew such relationships. These contacts help us in getting what we want in life. We know good manners, diligence, courtesy and goodwill are important for establishing good relationships with people. Yet, some times we feel like reading a crisp presentation of the rules that tell us a better way of doing it. Here are Ten Commandments of Human Relations recommended by American author Robert G. Lee:

- Speak to people. There is nothing as nice as a cheerful word of greeting.
- Smile at people. It takes seventy two muscles to frown, and only fourteen to smile.
- Call people by name. The sweetest music to anyone's ears is the sound of his/her own name.
- Be friendly and helpful. If you would have friends, be friendly.

- Be cordial, speak and act as if everything you do is a genuine pleasure.
- Be genuinely interested in people. You can like almost anybody if you try.
- Be generous with praise, and cautious with criticism.
- Be considerate with feelings of people. There are usually three sides to a controversy; yours, the other fellow's and the right one.
- Be alert to give service; what counts in life is what you do for others.
- Add to this a good sense of humour, a big dose of patience and a dash of humility and you will be rewarded manifold.

Business relationships for profit

Master-servant relationships still govern the employer-employee relationships; and they are highly valued because of their relationship with productivity. But more important are the business relationships with clients and customers. Corporate concern for relationship management is understandable, because profits are driven by business relationships. In *Business Psychology*, Leslie R. Beach and Elton L. Clark have given some helpful tips on how to maintain business relationships:

Understanding customer-dealer relationships
- The outlet or store is a service organisation.
- Customer wants prompt, courteous, and efficient service.
- Relationships with customer permeate all phases of business operations.
- The customer is usually a person with a problem.
- The customer's satisfaction greatly influences his general perception of and attitude towards the place of business.

Improving personal contacts
- Recognise the needs of the other person or group.
- Display friendliness and warmth.

- Develop sensitivity to other's reactions.
- Develop the habit of listening.
- Maintain an open mind.
- Select suitable language.
- Refrain from projecting personal needs and biases.
- Keep the conversation on the subject.
- Be alert for facts.
- Endeavour to close the conversation in a positive way.

Improving customer relations
- Improve understanding of human behaviour.
- Show sincere interest in the customer and his problem.
- Deal appropriately with the dissatisfied customer.
- Maintain customer contacts through follow up.
- Arrange special services.
- Make practical use of human relations principles.

Some general suggestions
- Treat each customer as an individual. People are different!
- Become genuinely interested in other people, customers and their problems.
- Be pleasant. Smile.
- Be a good listener. Encourage others to talk about themselves.
- Talk in terms of other man's interests.
- Realise that there is always a reason for an individual's behaviour and try to find out that reason.
- Recognise and appeal to strong drives in people.
- Don't make statements or promises to people that you can't back up. Most of the things people do are done because the person *feels* like doing them, not because he thinks it is the best.

Businessmen are eager to establish new business contacts and maintain customer relations to increase their market share. Most of their direct marketing strategies cover relationship management. They are looking for new ways to strengthen their relations with their clients and maintain lifetime relationships. In the process they want to capture business from clients and customers. "Building relationships is our biggest challenge," says Phiroz Vandrevala, vice-president of Tata Consultancy Services. Perhaps, he is speaking for the entire business community, because most of the businessmen feel the same way. It is the willingness to share the profits that enhances business relationships.

Life is nurtured by caring and sharing

We show our love and concern to our loved ones in many ways. We show how really we care by sharing what we can. In the same way getting along with people means being friendly, showing concern, loving and caring, and helping and giving. "When I give, I give my self," says American poet Walt Whitman. Yes, true caring means giving something of ours. In other words, real caring requires sharing what we have. To show care, concern and consideration to others is indeed a blessing, for we will receive it back tenfold.

Caring is in our blood

Caring and learning to be cared for starts early in childhood. Even babies get the reassurance that they are cared for, when parents talk—and they can ask for something and have their needs met. And when they begin to imitate their parents, they start caring for others. Caring is nurtured in our families and extended to the members of the society.

"Ours is a troubled and rapidly changing society," says American writer Aletha James Lindstrom in "Care a Little, Care a Lot" (*Reader's Digest*, March '81). "Yet one basic reality doesn't change: we humans are caring creatures. From birth to death we must care and be cared for. Otherwise we become lost, lonely souls, eventually seeking substitutes in anti-social behaviour, drugs or alcohol, psychosomatic illness, meaningless love affairs.

"Each of us can develop a capacity for caring if we make an honest effort. Habits of self-centeredness and indifference are hard to overcome. But if we daily make promise to ourselves to reach out to just one person, we have taken the first step. Next move will be easier.

"Your children may no longer need you. But there are many who do. Now is the time to find them. We must remember that there is no such thing as a small act of kindness or concern. If we just find one opportunity each day to make someone a little happier—and act upon it—the results can be impressive."

Many individuals and organisations are coming forward to care for deserving people. Even companies and corporate bodies are recognising the need for caring people. They are taking care of employees, by providing medical aid, recreational facilities, accident insurance, family welfare, etc.

Governments have recognised the need for taking care of deserving sections of the society. Women and child welfare programmes, hostels for orphans, schools for the blind, dumb and deaf, aid for the victims of natural calamities speak of the enormous importance being given to this aspect. Prime Minister Dr. Manmohan Singh, says that there was an overwhelming response from people all over the world to his call to help the victims of the 2004 Tsunami disaster. He expressed his gratitude by saying "Thank you for caring." Caring for the fellow beings is not only in our blood, it is in our upbringing. Yes, as Rabbi Harold Kushner puts it, "caring about others, running the risk of feeling, leaving an impact on people brings happiness."

Sharing gives meaning to life

We must give our all to form a satisfying relationship; and that is what we call sharing. Sharing behaviour—the process of give and take, reciprocating love, cooperation, and exchanging things has evolved in our interdependent society as a necessity for survival.

Researchers at the University of Pennsylvania recently found that vast majority of people, about 63 per cent, are reciprocators (people who are used to give and take), though we are all cooperators, free riders and reciprocators. In any group there are substantial number of reciprocators. Lead researcher Robert Kurzban points out that reciprocity is an important motive in human societal behaviour.

"The life of a person has meaning if it enriches the lives of people materially, intellectually and morally," says philosopher Albert Einstein. Yes, sharing is meaningful in our lives because it enriches life on earth.

Sharing knowledge and information

We love to acquire knowledge and enjoy sharing it with our loved ones. The profession of teaching is blessed with the noble activity of sharing knowledge with fellow beings. All educational institutions such as schools, colleges, universities are meant to serve this purpose. The media shares the information and knowledge. Books, newspapers, radio and talk shows on TV have the common function of updating us with the latest information on many events in the world.

Conversation is sharing personal views and knowledge

Conversation essentially is the socio-cultural give-and-take. It's a way of sharing of ideas through the medium of language. Communication is a way of getting through, whereas information is giving out. "Conversational give-and-take is among the most enjoyable and rewarding mental activities", says James Nathan Miller, a communication specialist. "Like study, it informs. Like travel, it broadens. Like friendship, it nourishes the soul. It calls, however, for a willingness to alternate the role of a speaker with that of a listener, and it calls for occasional 'digestive pauses' by both."

A good conversation is more than ferreting out information. It is a way of sharing personal views and ideas with friends. To enjoy a good conversation you require a few important skills: Ability to interact smoothly, sharp intellect, flawless ability to talk, clear pronunciation, soft voice and willingness to listen and learn. Good grooming, pleasing poise and graceful presentation will definitely add up, but they are not necessary.

American humorist Gelett Burgess gives ten simple rules to guide our conversation in "The Delightful Game of Conversation" (*Reader's Digest* July '67). They are as relevant today as ever:

- *Avoid social friction*
  " There is a fundamental principle underlying good talk," says Burgess. "The principle—the basis of all manners—is the avoidance of friction in social contacts, emotional friction caused by irritation, boredom, envy, egotism, or ridicule."
- *Avoid subjective talk.* Skip personal gossip. Avoid emotional friction.
- *Don't monopolise.* Speak succinctly; don't monopolise. Remember you are taking part in a social give-and-take. It is simple manners to allow others to express their views.
- *Don't contradict.* Never say "I don't agree."
- *Don't abruptly change the subject.* Don't divert the attention to introduce a new topic. Interruption can affect speaker's thought process. Reflect and digest what has been said.
- *Show active interest in what is said.* Ask questions to show your interest in what is being talked about. Your curious listening will bring out the best in the speaker.
- *After diversion, bring back the subject.* If you think that a subject is lost due to any cause you may reintroduce the forgotten topic. This will show your interest in the subject.
- *Don't make dogmatic statements of opinion.* You may speak anything but never with an expression of finality.

- *Avoid destructive talk.* Evil, of course, must be condemned. But never make a derogatory remark. It hurts.
- *Listen to the speaker with interest.* Listening is an opportunity to learn more about life. Indicate your interest in what the other person says, involve your whole body, and don't interrupt.

"A good listener strikes an effective balance of reflective paraphrasing and silent responsiveness," says Colleen McKenna in *Powerful Communication Skills.*

Love is behind sharing life

Interestingly the German word for love—*leiben,* differs from the word for life—*leben,* by only one letter " i ". Except for one letter the two words are almost identical. That speaks of the importance of love in man's life. Possibly, this is because life can not be complete without love. Behind most of our personal relationships, there is sharing of love—caring and being cared for. Love can be found in most unexpected places because every one deserves it. "I have felt and I have lived it and now it leaves me here; love is the ultimate pain and joy , without it you die with it you perish," says American writer Christopher S Dew.

In "Simple Secrets of Family Communication" (*Reader's Digest,* Feb.'87), Rhea Zakich says showing love is the most important ingredient in family relations. She gives some tips to improve communication among family members:
- Listen—just listen
- Don't criticise or judge
- Talk from heart
- Don't assume
- Show your love

A glimmer of hope in sharing

It has been said man can live about forty days without food, and three days without water, and about eight minutes without air, and only one second without hope. Dr Victor Frankl, an Austrian psychiatrist, observes in *Man's Search for Meaning*, that a prisoner in a German concentration camp did not continue to live long after hope was lost. But even the slightest ray of hope, the rumour of better food, a whisper about escape helped some of the camp inmates to continue living even under systematic horror.

Hope can enliven the spirits and encourage the desire to live. It is hope that reassures the desperate ones, that encourages people to share what they have. "Hope is itself a species of happiness," says British author Samuel Johnson; "and perhaps, the chief happiness which this world affords."

Sharing makes a difference in the world

"It is not by accident that the happiest people are those who make a conscious effort to live useful lives. Their happiness, of course, is not shallow exhilaration where life is one continuous intoxicating party. Rather, their happiness is a deep sense of inner peace that comes when they believe their lives have meaning and that they are making a difference for good in the world," says Bishop Earnest A Fitzgerald.

We learn the inner secret of happiness when we learn to direct our inner drives, our interests and our attention to something outside ourselves. Remember that the happiest people are not those getting more but those giving more. Share what you have and make a difference in the world.

Sharing happiness is a spiritual experience

"To have joy one must share it; happiness was born a twin," says British poet Lord Byron. Happiness seems to be shared. "Happiness quite unshared, can scarcely be called happiness, it has no taste," observes British novelist Charlotte Bronte. "You are forgiven for your happiness and success only if you generously share them," says Nobel laureate Albert Camus. Happiest are the people who give most happiness to others. Share the joy of happiness. Share the joy of living.

"Happiness is spiritual, born of truth and love. It is unselfish and, therefore cannot exist alone: but requires all mankind to share it," observes Mary Baker Eddy, the founder of Christian Science. "If you do a good job for others, you heal yourself at the same time, because a dose of joy is a spiritual cure," says American writer Thomas Edward Bodett.

Sharing life with family members

"To be happy at home is the ultimate end to which every enterprise and labour tends, and of which every desire prompts the prosecution," says British author Samuel Johnson. Yes, family is the main source of happiness for every human being. No joy in the world equals the bliss of living with one's own family.

Sharing life with parents and elders

We honour our parents for their lifetime service. Your father is responsible for bringing you into this world. He gave you identity and family name. He is the one who teaches you about life and guides you all through. He is the hero you emulate in our life. "My father is my hero," thinks every child.

The sound "mamma" has the same meaning in many languages. The word 'mother' transcends all cultures in the world because only a mother can give life. The image of mother nestles in the heart of every human being on earth, simply because we owe our birth to her. Before the loving care of a mother, no parallel exists in the world; it is so exclusive, endearing and overwhelming that no one can afford to forget it, ever. A mother is a child's icon, a divine object of emulation. She helps the child to realise its dreams.

Whatever you wanted and whenever needed it, she was always there with you. Without her nurturing love, constant care, sharing life, your childhood memories would not have been that sweet. Even in those difficult years of growing up, she was with you all the while, catering to your needs, attending to your problems, correcting mistakes, seeing through your adolescent dilemmas, guiding and directing you to do the right things at the right time.

We have a special relationship with our parents, that hasn't happened overnight. It has come through years of learning, sharing and growing. We know there have been times in our lives when we had trouble accepting the things, they were trying to teach us. When we thought they were being too strict or old fashioned. When we thought they didn't understand. But we have come to realise that they understood all along, that they were guiding us, not only with love but with their experience as parents. Because of the way they have cared, we have now become better persons. We know we are better prepared to meet whatever happens in life. They have always been there when we needed them and they have certainly filled our lives with many bright and happy moments, which we keep in our fondest memory.

Now as grown-ups, we feel so much closer to our parents. And more and more we find new ways to share life, new ways to relate to them, and new feelings to share. We know we have so much in common, as adults, as friends, and so much to look forward to in the years ahead. Their love touches us every day. We are grateful in our hearts for many kind deeds and helpful things they have done for us over the years, and their loving relationships means so much to us.

Sharing wonderful moments with spouse

Everybody needs a life partner. Choosing a spouse is not that easy. In most cases the choice is made either by love or by arrangement. Whatever the way it is, choose once and choose well, because it is for a lifetime. Greek philosopher Socrates says, "By all means marry. If you get a good wife you will be happy; if you get a bad one you become a philosopher." We may have to replace the word 'wife' with 'spouse,' so that we get a broader meaning that includes husbands as well.

Marriage is a civil arrangement between the opposite sex to live together for a lifetime. It caters to the natural urge of sex and conjugal bliss during the youthful and active years. Blissful moments of togetherness bring happiness and contentment in married life. But more than that it is a balancing act between parents, children, friends and a career. It offers unlimited joy of family life till the end. The running theme of marital happiness is the sharing of life with the loved ones. "Love is the condition in which the happiness of another person is essential to your own," says American author Robert Heinlein. When the loving person is your spouse, no joy can surpass the bliss of married life.

"Marriage is an adventure," says Shobhaa De, the celebrity writer, a devout wife and mother of six, in her book *Spouse: The Truth about Marriage*. " It's about trust, companionship, affection and sharing." The greatest bliss of marital relationship is in togetherness. It begins with a bloom of intense romantic intimacies that ultimately creates an enduring bond of partnership throughout life. It is the most blessed relationship that promises enduring joy in every person's life. Its essence is in sharing life with the partner. Sharing love immortalises the marital relationship between the couples and acknowledges the realities of existence. To love and to be loved is the greatest happiness in the world for many people. "The entire sum of existence is the magic of being needed by just one person," says American author Vi Putnam.

Psychologist Norbert Schwarz and his colleagues at the University of Michigan reported in a recent article published in *Science*, that intimate relations form the most enjoyable part of life. Yes, sex is important in life because you enjoy it. The ability to enjoy sex may decline with age; yet couples continue to live a happily married life till they die. The simple reason is that sex isn't everything in life; there are other important love ingredients that bless the married life. Human beings are greatly blessed in sharing love and joy with spouse. Sharing love is not limited to the couple; it extends naturally to all the members of the family. Yes, there is not a single day when we do not think of our loved ones.

In "Bring Fun Back to Your Marriage" (*Reader's Digest,* May '89), Marriage Counsellors Edwin Kiester Jr., and Sally Valente Kiester give a few tips for a happy marital relationship:

- *Let your guard down* — Don't work your marriage as a cheerless routine. You don't have to be guarded. Don't guard your cheerfulness.
- *Plan to be spontaneous* — Do whatever you like, spontaneously. Carve time for both of you. Spend some time together.
- *Be playful* — Have a good time together in play. Playful intimacy is something that transcends time and age.
- *Surprise each other* — Doing something unexpected for your spouse shows that you have been thinking of him/her. A surprise says, "You have been in my thoughts while we were apart."
- *Laugh together* — Recharge your relationship with mirth. Enjoy laughing together.
- *Bring joy back to your sex life.* — Fun is important in marital life. "The best marriages have lightheartedness." Variety must be the spice of sex.

"A marriage thrives on the sunlight of familiarity and routine, but the water of novelty is also needed to keep the relationship from withering."

Sharing clarity becomes the healing

"Healing hurt feelings is another art that can be learnt in intimate relationships," says psychotherapist Tina Tessina in *It Ends With You*. "Human beings are imperfect and clumsy. We often stumble and hurt each other. The closer we get, the more likely we are to bruise each other emotionally. It is almost guaranteed that your feelings will be hurt in any intimate relationship. With practice, you learn to heal yourself individually and you and your partner can work together, to heal each other.

"Whenever you are hurt or upset in a relationship situation ....discover its source, and get as clear as you can. Find out where your hurt comes from. Once you understand your hurt feelings, share them gently with your partner. No accusations. Simply a statement of experience.

"Sometimes, sharing clarity becomes the healing. After sharing and talking, figure out a way to protect yourself next time. You'll find that as soon as you know how to protect yourself, all the hurt and anger fade quickly."

Caring children and grandchildren: sharing joy

Children feel that no one loves better than mummy and daddy, because they know how dearly they look after. One loving embrace can make a child feel secure. One word of appreciation makes him feel on top of the world. Without parents, life seems impossible. Our parents are the first people who taught us how to be happy in this world. In *Making Happy People* American author Paul Martin says, "Happiness is arguably the most important thing in the world." He discusses how we can bring up our children to be happy.

A kiss or hug can reinforce love, and make children happy. "Did you hug your child today?," asks American author Arlene Silberman. " It is a question many parents find unsettling. But—for the well-being of your children—think about it." Love your children and teach them how to love.

Whenever we see a child, we are flooded with our childhood memories. The child in you makes you join the gang ; you feel like playing like a child once again. If the child happens to be your own son or daughter, you feel like sharing your childhood experiences. You feel like teaching what you have learned in childhood. You combine teaching while entertaining them with play. To nurture their curiosity, you weave fairy tales or stories of adventure of legendary heroes and heroines. It builds their character and sows seeds of achievement. Thus you can help them dream things to do when they grow up.

Joy in upbringing
If a bright boy is making poor grades at a highly competitive school, his parents might consider transferring him to another school that provides more nurturing environment. Or if a teacher complains that a girl seems distracted by her constant scribbling, the parent might want to enroll the child in an arts class instead of inadvertently killing her creative efforts.

And if they are your grandchildren, you certainly enjoy their naughty antics and mischievous behaviour, giggling smiles and gurgling laughter. You often join them in sharing fun . Sharing joy with children and grandchildren begins with teaching them the right conduct—how to behave well. You feel like teaching them the most urgent things first—the do's and don'ts in particular. The most important things are manners, courtesy, cooperation, respect, compassion, helpfulness. Teach them positive values in life, that help us live a happy life.

"First, teach a child to be happy," says American author Ardis Whitman in "Five enduring values for your child" (*Reader's Digest* Dec '81). "Happiness is by no means life's greatest goal, and it is not necessary to be happy all the time. But the habit of being pleased has sustained many a broken heart." She also thinks that we must teach children, the importance of love, honesty, courage, and faith, besides happiness.

Our earnest desire to share life makes us talk to growing children; it is never a wasted time. Sharing life with adolescent members of the family is very crucial for their development. Their need to find and establish their own identity is foremost during this stage; while fears of ridicule and need for acceptance bother them a lot. Since we have passed through that stage, we are better qualified to understand their problems. We need to listen to their problems with sympathy, understand their challenges, respect their concerns and accept their frustrations. It is our duty to discuss their problems frankly and help them make successful adults. We must act wisely, if not as role models, by sharing the realities of life. Remember that their peers and friends dominate their emotional landscape; they are crucial to help make successful transition from adolescence to adulthood. More than the help we offer, it is the sharing of our adolescent experiences that does the trick.

Sharing joy and sorrow with friends, relatives and neighbours

Relatives are the members of our extended family, whereas our friends are the family we choose. They are our links with the society outside the family. We all require support of the people around us for our survival. Professor Robert Kurzban of the University of Pennsylvania says that reciprocity is a an important motive in human societal behaviour. We all reciprocate good relations; and we are willing to share what we have. Therefore, we must learn to have a good network of friends and relatives and strengthen our relationships. We must keep the bridges open and maintain hot line connectivity all the time; because we never know when we need them. Sharing life with significant people in our lives is, perhaps, the best way to ensure this.

Friends: the family we choose
"What is a friend? A single soul dwelling in two bodies," says Greek philosopher Aristotle. Former US President Thomas Jefferson compared friendship to wine—it's a "restorative." Yes, like a good wine, friendship can give you a lift, it lasts. Inclement conditions destroy it.

We all know the value of close friends since childhood. We shared our personal secrets and private sufferings with them. We needed them whenever we wanted to share our joys and sorrows. We learned a lot of things from our friends. Even when we grew up we continued to look up for their friendship, help and support whenever we were in need. " I cannot imagine where I would be today were it not for that handful of friends who have given me a heart full of joy," says devotional writer Charles R. Swindol. "Let's face it , friends make life a lot more fun."

Deep friendship between people is an urgent need in the world today. People seek friendship hungrily. We all would like to fortify our lives with our friendships. " Be courteous to all, but intimate with few," advises first US President George Washington. "And let those few be well tried, before you give them your confidence. True friendship is like a plant of slow growth and must undergo and withstand the shocks of adversity before it is entitled to appellation." "The secret of happiness is this," says British philosopher Betrand Russell, "let your interests be as wide as possible, and let your reactions to things and persons be as friendly rather than hostile."

Friendship: the secret to longer life

It is sharing of life that grows friendly relations. Friendship is essentially caring and sharing. It is nourished by faith, nurtured by trust and reinforced by give and take. It is not what we take from others but what we give —not so much in material gifts as the gifts of compassion, sincerity, understanding. It is instilling faith and courage in others.

It is transfer of our self-respect to others. It is the sharing of our confidence with others.

It is meeting them more than half way, giving the best we are promoting the good and happiness we have. As Roman orator Marcus Tullius Cicero puts it, " Friendship improves happiness and abates misery, by doubling our joy and dividing our grief."

How to win friends

If you know the art of friendship, you can prolong your life. It puts a smile of contentment on your self image. Success Guru Dale Carnegie's *How to Win Friends and Influence People* has been read for six decades now. The principles he gave are relevant even today:
- Be genuinely interested in people
- Make them feel important and appreciated
- Listen intently with genuine interest
- Get the other person's point of view
- Talk about what the other person wants, and show how to get it
- Let the other person discover it himself
- Avoid arguments
- Emphasise on things you both agree
- Kindliness, friendly approach and appreciation can win people

Have a good network of close friends

"Better to have a hundred friends than a 100 rubies," says a Russian saying. "Have social contacts , a good network of friends," says American writer Laura Cartensen. "Most crucial is having close friends –the kind of people you can't imagine life without. Quality beats the quantity all the time."

Friends should be reliable and dependable. Demand for trustworthy people never diminishes in this uncertain world. Associate with good people and be amiable and friendly. Project yourself as a friendly person. Be honest and build trust; do what you say. If you can't meet promises, never come up with alibis or excuses. Don't ever make meaningless promises that you can't do.

"You find yourself refreshed in the presence of cheerful people, why not make an honest effort to confer that pleasure on others?" says American author Lydia M. Child. "Half the battle is won if you never allow yourself to say anything gloomy." American poet Amanda Bradley says, "Celebrate the happiness the friends are always giving. Make every day a holiday and celebrate just living."

Archbishop Thomas Davidson puts a rider on friendships: "Associate with noble people you can find, read the best books, live with the mighty. But learn to be happy alone. Rely upon your energies, so do not wait for or depend on other people."

Be thankful for sharing with friends

Here one is reminded of a beautiful thanksgiving prayer from Avery Brooke's "Plain Prayers for a Complicated World" (*Reader's Digest*, May '89): "O God, thank you for my friends and all the joys they have brought. I thank you for the happiness of sharing work and problems and laughter, and for the joy of adventuring and learning together. I thank you for the chance to love and be loved, not because of cleverness or goodness but in spite of faults and differences."

Forgive and give: the secret of retaining friends
In our eagerness to share life with friends, we make some mistakes; most of the time they are unintended. This happens because of the differences in upbringing, family values, perceptions, traditions and attitudes and interests. Because of misunderstanding, our friends appear to be doing wrong things to us. "It takes a great soul to be a true friend," says Anna Robertson Brown. "One must forgive much , forget much, and forbear much." "A friend should bear a friend's infirmities," writes Shakespeare in *Julius Caesar*. We must learn to forgive our friends. "He who cannot forgive others breaks the bridge over which he must pass himself" says philosopher George Herbert. " Keep a fair sized back yard to bury the faults of your friends," advises Clergyman Henry Ward Beacher.

It takes more than forgiveness to rebuild and retain friendship. We must learn to forgive our friends; only then our friendship can have true value. "Forgiving transforms bitterness into neutrality or even into positively tinged memories and so makes much greater life satisfaction possible," says Psychologist Martin E P Seligman. "You can't hurt the perpetrator by not forgiving, but you can set yourself free by forgiving. Physical health, particularly in cardiovascular terms , is likely to be better in those who forgive than in those who do not. And when it is followed by reconciliation, forgiving can vastly improve your relations with the person forgiven. (It's worth to surrender a grudge)."

Our neighbour is also a human being capable of making errors that distort his perspective. He can mistakenly feel that you are his enemy, not his friend. You forgive. Everyone seeks forgiveness as ardently as he seeks food or shelter. Yet, we are ashamed to make a mistake, as if it were a terrible weakness to make a mistake or forgive.

Unforgiven acts of people weigh so heavily on us that they shatter the brain and strain the mind. The pressure of stress is so great that it tries to explode any time. The moment we forgive people, our heart is relieved of the heavy burden of guilt. Peace comes back to mind and health resumes.

In a study published in *Harvard Women's Health Watch* it has been reported that the old adage 'forgive and forget' not only makes you happier it also makes you healthier. It has been found that forgiving people reduces stress, makes your heart rate improve, and also keeps your blood pressure under control. On the other hand, nursing a grudge can induce bodily strains, tense muscles, elevated blood pressure, and increased sweating. The study found a link between forgiving and improvement in health.

Be in touch with old friends
Bonhomie, the good natured geniality and friendliness, is necessary not only to establish rapport but also to maintain contacts in the society. We must always be in touch with our friends and maintain connectivity. Many of our friendships need a little nurturing to help them flourish. Consultant Jan Yager, the author of *Friendshifts* and *When Friendship Hurts*, tells us how to catch up with old friends:

- Stop feeling guilty that you can't spend lot of time with old friends, like you did long time ago. Acknowledge that your lives have changed, and do whatever you can now to maintain the relationship. Use e-mail, instant messaging and other electronic devices to stay in touch when you have small bits of time.
- Meet for coffee or early morning walk before you start your working day.
- Schedule regular "friends out" in which you set aside one-week night a month, for example, to catch up with your buddies.

- Invite your friends to share everyday activities you normally do alone, like exercising, doing errands, or going to your kid's soccer game.
- Try to be there for key events in your friend's life—weddings, graduations, funerals. Your presence will make a difference.

Relatives and neighbours: our extended family

We need relatives to share our joys and sorrows. We invite them to take part in our joys; and no happy occasion is complete without their presence. They grace the occasion whenever there is a joyful event in the family. Remember those happy occasions when we share our joys—marriages, baby showers, birthday parties, cradle ceremonies, family celebrations.

Our relatives are our contacts and links with the outside world. And they are the people who visit us whenever there is an unhappy event in the family. They are the people who provide emotional support when it is badly needed to uphold our spirits: accidents, sufferings, death in the family, etc. Relatives do influence how we feel and think.

Relations with neighbours are a must for peaceful living. They are the people who are available in times of need; and they are the people who share their life with us. It is the give and take relationship that strengthens the neighbourly relations. Sharing life enhances understanding; help and cooperation results in long-term relationships with neighbours. Harmonious relationships lead to secure surroundings and peaceful neighbourhood.

Sharing life with fellow human beings

The society we live in is full of people we don't know much about. We are often influenced by our likes and dislikes, and prejudices, that makes us hate strange people. Our reactions are quite natural in a world filled with corrupt politicians with cockeyed ideologies, religious fanatics with dogmatic doctrines, confused terrorists and brainwashed suicide bombers, cut-throat criminals with no respect for law, business men looking for profits, social workers with ulterior motives, and plenty of self-centred people.

But then you don't have to isolate yourself like English novelist Daniel Defoe's Robinson Crusoe in a remote island without people. You don't have to be a cynical loner hanging on the edge. Remember, you are living in a society, where interdependence, give and take and sharing life are the normal ways of living. Here everyone has to depend on others for survival. Come, join the crowd, discover how comfortable is the company of fellow beings. Find how enjoyable are the activities of sharing life.

Sharing diffuses anger

When we meet people with a lot of expectations, unconsciously we often make unrelenting demands on them. Sometimes they don't meet our expectations, for some reason or the other. As it hurts our ego, our immediate reaction is anger. You are angry with people, who you think have hurt you. Suddenly the unexpected encounter is seen as a threatening situation. We perceive a threat to our being—a physical hurt or psychological threat. But we don't know what is threatening or why it is dangerous. As fear continues to haunt us, we are engulfed by anger and anxiety.

As a normal person it is natural to be angry when badly mistreated. Our immediate reaction is to fight back and show the world what you can do. But whatever happens, don't lash out aggressively. If the offending person is a stranger, stay away from him. If the other person is someone you cannot avoid, let him/her know calmly, what is bothering you and why. Tell him so right away, without offending. This approach provides an opportunity for the other person to understand you.

Sharing a perceived threat diffuses your anger. Personal anger must be shared with someone close to you—a friend, spouse, or relative. Let him/ her know that you recognise the threat and you intend to control your anger. This will clarify your perceptions and reduce the intensity of your bad feelings. It permits you to receive feedback from your well-wishers and their consensual validation. Sharing also implies trust, kindness and forgiveness. Forgive yourself and others for the misunderstanding or what caused your anger. Cancel charges and forget the perceived wrong. Open your friendly heart for future transactions.

Sharing resolves conflicts

Whenever two or more people come together, conflicts of interest are common in our society. This is natural because we are different persons with varying cultural backgrounds and value systems, interests, needs and choices. In most cases the root cause of conflict lies in bruised egos or failed communication. So, don't allow your self-esteem to be dragged into the issue.

A conflict is, in fact, a welcome piece of irony. It promises peace if you can resolve it, otherwise hell. Interpersonal issues continue to persist unless resolved by an earnest dialogue. A meaningful debate is an open discussion where everyone can frankly express personal views and convey disagreement or dissent, if any. Avoid "them" and "us" kind of attitude, while dealing with conflicts. Realise that only "us" and "us" kind of thinking can lead to win/win situations. Any effort to reduce conflicts should follow some sensible approach:

Establish rapport before you negotiate

Good manners, politeness, courtesy, kindness, and friendliness are necessary prerequisites for any encounter. Remember, you decide how people will treat you, it is not the other way round.

Be tolerant and accommodative

Accommodate the emotional outbursts of the opposite party. Don't react emotionally.

Be cooperative
"In any negotiation both sides want to win, so look for creative approach," says Stephen Kozicki in *The Creative Negotiator.* "Approach your negotiation in a spirit of fairness and cooperation, genuinely wanting both sides to win . By doing this you can ensure that the negotiation truly embraces the deliberate style on the continuum."

Keep common interests in mind
We live in an interdependent society, where our happiness depends on happiness of all. Think of common good.

Discuss common problems
Be issue centered. Be willing to listen. Get other's point of view. Understand the core of the problem. Look for available options agreeable to both parties. Allay fears of consequences of proposed actions. Highlight the common benefits.

Our survival depends on sharing strategies
Key to resolving conflicts lies in give-and-take attitudes. Give what you can, and take what others give.

Be willing to sacrifice
Happiness and satisfaction may not come without a price. Be ready to sacrifice what you can. Resulting benefits could be substantial for both the parties.

Arrive at a consensus
Create a win-win situation for both the parties. Work out a plan of action and the modalities for implementing them.

Efforts towards resolving conflicts may not always lead to win-win situations. Instead they may end up like a zero-sum game where gains and losses match each other, resulting in status quo position. In rare unfortunate situations, they may create lose-lose consequences for both the parties. "Even if you lose you will be the ultimate winner of long-term relationship," says Kozicki; "You will have respect and reputation not only for fairness, but for creativity in proposing win-win solutions." Even if you lose, you win!

Lastly take Ann Lander's advice, as given in "Coping with Crises" (*Reader's Digest,* April '81): "Expect trouble as an inevitable part of life and, when it comes, look squarely in the eye and say, 'I will be bigger than you. You cannot defeat me.' Then repeat yourself the most comforting of all words, 'This too shall pass'."

Sharing happy moments with the unfortunate ones

Share what you can

You are much more able to cope with sadness, better if you have some happiness in your life. If you can share a bit of happiness, you are helping the people to help themselves. Come share your fare, no matter how meagre it is; for there are millions of deserving people who don't even have a fraction of what you have. Increase your happiness by taking away the wretchedness of others. Here you better read what some wise people have said:

> "So much sadness exists in the world that we are under obligation to contribute as much joy as lies within our powers."
>
> *Dr John Sutherland Bonnel, Presbyterian pastor*

> "Whatever mitigates the woes or increases the happiness of others is a just criterion of goodness and whatever injures society at large or any individual in it is a criterion of inequity."
>
> *Oliver Goldsmith, British author*

> "There is no way to be completely happy without being oblivious to the world around you."
>
> *Meredith Close, American author*

"When you have seen the glow of happiness on the face of a beloved person, you know that a man can have no vacation but to awaken that light on the faces surrounding him ; and you are torn by the thought of unhappiness and night you cast, by the mere fact of living, in the hearts you encounter."
Albert Camus, a Nobel laureate

"One of the things I keep learning is that the secret of happiness is doing things for others."
Dick Gregory, American artist

"If we try hard to bring happiness to others, we cannot stop it from coming to us also."
Sir John Templeton, Philanthropist

"Life is short, whenever you have enough time for gladdening the hearts of those who travel with us, be swift to love."
Henri Frederick Amiel, Swiss writer

"To serve is beautiful, but only if it is done with joy and whole heart and a true mind."
Pearl S. Buck, Nobel laureate

"Consciously or unconsciously one renders some service or the other. If we cultivate the habit of doing this service deliberately, our desire for service will steadily grow stronger, and it will make not only for our happiness, but that of the world at large."
Mahatma Gandhi

"There are those who give with joy,
And that joy will be their reward."
Kahlil Gibran, Lebanese philosopher

"Little deeds of kindness
Little words of love
Help to make the earth happy
Like the heaven above."
Julia Carney, American poet

Happiness is sharing joy with others

"Happiness is a sun beam which may pass through a thousand bosoms without losing its original ray; nay, when it strikes on a kindred heart, like the converged light on a mirror, it reflects with redoubled brightness. It is not perfect till it is shared," says American novelist Jane Porter. Happiness is a hard thing because it is achieved by making others happy. We feel happy when we share our joy with other fellow beings. As Sir James M. Barrie says, "Those who bring sunshine into the lives of others cannot keep it from others."

"To get joy we must give it, and to keep joy we must scatter it," says philanthropist Sir John Templeton. "Your happiness increases the more you give your happiness away," says Professor Dr. Bruce Bogart. We all know that by sharing joy with others we virtually distribute happiness. We all spend joyful moments with our friends and family members on many occasions. Several things come to mind—fun and frolic of the colourful holidays; sparkling nights of Diwali; joyful days of Baisakhi, merry times of Christmas, New Year and Pongal. French novelist Honore de Balzac says, "Someday you will find that there is far more happiness in another's happiness than in your own. It is something I cannot explain, something within that sends a glow of warmth all through you."

Share smiles: light up lives with fun and laughter!

We usually express our happiness through smiles and laughs. In fact, a smile is an effortless way to share happiness. It is said that it is easier to smile than frown because it takes fourteen muscles to smile and seventy-two to frown.

"A smile costs nothing but it gives much," says an anonymous author. "It enriches those who receive without making poorer those who give. It takes but a moment, but the memory of it sometimes lasts forever. None is so rich or mighty that he can get along without it and none so poor that he can be made rich by it. A smile creates happiness in the home, fosters goodwill in business and is the countersign of friendship. It brings rest to the weary, cheer to the discouraged, sunshine to the sad, and nature's best antidote for trouble. Yet it cannot be bought, begged, borrowed or stolen, for it is something that is of no value to anyone until it is given away. Some people are too tired to give you a smile. Give them one of yours, as none needs a smile so much as who has no more to give."

"Man is distinguished from all other creations by the faculty of laughter," says American author Joseph Addison. "Mirth is like a flash of lightning that breaks through the gloom of clouds and glitters for a moment." This is, indeed, one quality that makes us special, because no other living being is capable of laughing. It is a vehicle for expression of our joyful feelings, and happiness in life.

You will be cheerful because you smile and laugh. "Cheerfulness is the best promoter of health and is as friendly to the mind as to the body," says Joseph Addison. Your own laughter will make you feel better. "Hysterical laughter is a good sign. Releases nervous tension. Relieves frustrations," says Will Stanton (*Reader's Digest,* Sept. '68). It is indeed an antidote for anger and stress. Our smiles and laughs help us in keeping ourselves healthy. Few persons realise that health actually varies according to the amount of laughter. According to American writer Peter Michelmore (*Reader's Digest,* June '84), "The foundations of good health lie in love, laughter, and faith in oneself." "People who laugh live longer than people who don't laugh," says artist James S Walsh. The same point is repeated by a Norwegian proverb: "He who laughs, lasts."

No matter how much madder it may make you, get out of the bed and smile. You may not smile because you are not cheerful;

but if you force yourself to smile you end up laughing. "Repeated experiments prove that when a man assumes the facial expressions of a given mental mood—any mood—then that mood itself will follow," says psychologist Kenneth Goode. Light up your face with smile. Forget the rigours of life, for a while, with a hearty laugh. Let the stream of laughter purify your soul. Share mad, giddy laughter with family and friends. American poet Ella Wheeler Wilcox says, "Laugh, the world laughs with you; Weep, and you weep alone; For the sad old earth has to borrow its mirth; It has trouble enough of its own."

"To laugh often and much, to win respect of intelligent people and affection of children, to leave the world a better place, to know even one life has breathed easier because you have lived. This is to have succeeded," says American author Ralph Waldo Emerson. He insists that we should learn to smile and laugh as often as we can because that is the essence of joyful living. "I want to tell you to keep laughing," says American writer Alan Alda (*Reader's Digest,* Dec.'81). "You gurgle when you laugh. Be sure to laugh three times a day for your own well-being. And if you can get other people to join you in your laughter, you may help keep this shaky world afloat. When people are laughing, they're generally not killing one another. Above all, laugh and enjoy your life of your own choosing and in a world of your making." Just as you pave the way with flowers, sprinkle smiles on your life path. Welcome life with all its joyful grandeur.

6

Love What You Do: Enjoy Work

Choose a job you love, and you will never have to work a day in your life.

Confucius (551-479 BC)
Chinese philosopher,

I feel that you are justified in looking into the future with true assurance, because you have a mode of living in which the joy of life and the joy of work are harmoniously combined. Add to this the spirit of ambition which pervades your being and seems to make day's work as a child at play.

Albert Einstein (1879 –1955)
Physicist, philosopher
Nobel prize for physics 1921

We, human beings can do anything
We are better equipped to achieve many things in this short life. Everyone of us has the urge to do something remarkable. Everybody wants to show the world what one can do. "What really distinguishes this generation in all countries is its determination to act, its joy in action, the assurance of being able to change things by one's own efforts," says American political scientist Hannah Arendt.

"What makes people happy is activity, changing evil itself into good by power, working in a moral manner," says German philosopher Johann Wolfgang Von Goethe. Of course, it is our mind that decides what is good or what is right. Whatever we do is good and right if we believe in it. We can do anything if we are determined to do it. In doing what we like we can find our own rhythm of life.

Find your calling

We all look for joyful preoccupation with satisfying work. That is the reason why we human beings spend more than half of our waking hours in the work we do. Sometimes we refer to it as calling, but there is a difference. Individuals with a calling see their work as contributing to the greater good, to something larger than they are. The work is fulfilling in its own right, without regard for money or advancement. When the money stops, promotions end, the work goes on. Traditionally callings are reserved to very prestigious and rarified work—priests, physicians and scientists. Professor Amy Wrzesniewski (pronounced rez-NES-kee) and her colleagues at the New York University discovered that any job can become a calling and any calling can become a job. "A physician who views the work as a job and is simply interested in making a good income does not have a calling, while a garbage collector who sees the work as making the world a cleaner, healthier place could have a calling."

"I really think happiness is closely aligned with success and may almost be interchangeable synonym. Happiness (like success) also comes from doing what we feel called to do in life; However it is also obvious that no one can experience one without the other," says American author Donna Fargo. If you are looking for a calling in life listen to Anna Robertson Brown, an enlightened American writer: "Ask yourself, is the work vital , strengthening my own character, or inspiring others, or helping the world."

Do whatever you are good at: take delight in what you achieve
It is delightful to listen to what wise people have said about work:

> " When you work you are a flute through whose heart the whispering of the hours turns to music."
> *Kahlil Gibran, Lebanese philosopher*

> "No other technique for the conduct of life attaches the individual firmly to reality as laying emphasis on work; for this work at least gives him secure place in a portion of reality, in the community."
> *Sigmund Freud, Austrian psychiatrist*

> "The grand essentials to happiness in life are something to do, something to love, and something to hope for."
> *Joseph Addison, American writer*

> "Happiness is bound up with the ability to work and to be readily interested in the world around you."
> *June Callwood, American writer*

> "Happiness or unhappiness of rational animal depends not on what he feels but what he does; just as virtue and vice consist not in feeling but doing."
> *Marcus Aurelius Antoninus, Roman emperor*

> "To fill the hour—that is happiness."
> *Ralph Waldo Emerson, American author*

> "Always leave enough time in your life to do something that makes you happy, satisfied, and even joyous. That has more of an effect on economic well-being than any single activity."
> *Paul Hawken, American author*

Advantages in doing what you like
Joy comes from exercising our creative powers. Open your eyes and explore new areas of endeavour. Concentration on something you like will fill your world with pleasure. Whatever you like,

do it with discipline, patience and practice. Remember, improvement is within your reach, not perfection. Consider the advantages:
- You are free to do what you like.
- You are your own boss.
- Enough scope for initiative and adventure.
- You have the discretion, you take the decisions.
- No external pressure; you work at your own pace.
- You are responsible for your actions; not accountable to anyone.
- You can have privacy, nobody to comment up on.
- You can realise your dreams, achieve goals, at your own pace.
- It fills your world with joy and pleasure.

Work gives you identity and security

Rani Mukherjee, a Bollywood actress made a profound statement in a televised interview (Dec. 19, 2004) with Simi Garewal: "Your friends and relatives respect you as a person because they know what you really are; but the entire world respects you because of your work. Work gives you name, fame, money, recognition and respect; and above all it establishes your identity in the world." It is indeed true.

Key to a satisfying job is in the security it offers. In a recent study, professor Francis Green and his colleagues at the University of Kent found that, "the most satisfied employee is one who is in a secure job, with a high level of individual discretion and participation in decision-making, but not requiring high intensity of work."

The reasons are obvious. A secure job offers a definite source of income, while there is no fear of unemployment. "Work hard, save money and collect retirement" is an old timer's motto. But the times have changed; modern man is after any job that gives him faster growth and greater benefits.

Show integrity in what you do

"When at work, be totally focused on it; and when it is your time don't think about work at all," says American author Judith M. Bardwick in *Seeking the Calm in the Storm*. She says one must make distinction between personal time-space and the official one. That is an important point in work integrity. People with integrity believe that hard work and honesty will bring just rewards.

This integrity comes from doing what we have to do. Oprah Winfrey, the famous TV anchor says, "Real integrity is doing the right thing, knowing that nobody is going to know you did it or not." When we say integrity, it is uncompromising honesty, personal as well as intellectual. "If you have integrity nothing else matters," says Alan Simpson. "If you don't have integrity nothing else matters."

Take charge of your working time

Your life is nothing but the time you spend between birth and death. You have only so much of it that you cannot afford to waste it. Time management experts Amy Bjork Harris and Dr. Thomas Harris give some tips as to how to make the best use of time (*Reader's Digest*, Feb. '86).

- We lose quantities of time by not being able to find things we want. "A place for everything and everything in its place," is a useful adage. Clutter really means unfinished time-consuming business. Develop systems to keep things in place.
- Never try to do too many things at a time. Better planning is the key to saving us much time and aggravation.
- Days can be wasted getting out of tasks we shouldn't have taken on. We know we don't have the time and that other commitments are still uncompleted, but when asked we still say yes. Never make a decision on the spur of the moment. Don't commit for job you can't handle.

- Unsolved problems can rob you of commitment to your work and reduce your precious free time. The question is not whether you have problems, but if they are the same ones you had for months or a year ago. If so, how many energy sapping hours have gone into worrying about them? Can't you resolve some of your quandaries and get on with your life?
- "Treasure your time, and plan its use well," say Harris and Harris. "You will like yourself –and your life."

Depend on your skill and effort—not luck

Pleasure is behind every skilled work. It gives an opportunity to make use of the inner talents and acquired skills. Skill-based earnings are soul-satisfying; they increase our self-confidence. Prefer games of skill, not games of luck. Earnings based on luck are not lasting. Easy come easy go. Anything that comes easily without skill or effort slips away like quick silver. Hard work is an amalgam of perseverance and effort. It is bound up with lasting happiness that comes from satisfying work.

Seek joy in excellence: learn to do well

"The secret of joy in work is contained in one word—excellence. To know how to do well is to enjoy it," says Nobel laureate Pearl S.Buck. Excellence expresses itself in a job well done. You will probably find that doing things really well is more ego enhancing than doing a lot less effectively. Therefore, whatever you do, learn to do well; and you will soon find yourself doing excellent things that bring out joy in work. To excel your own previous performance should be your aim. Remember, the real competition is between your previous performance and your present effort to excel.

"Society has its own definitions of success... such as status, fame, money, and power," says Geet Sethi, seven times World Billiards Champion in his recent book *Success vs Joy*. He says

"Success is a result. It is a job well done. When I wanted success and was willing to sacrifice joy for it, I eventually got neither." According to him "the road to excellence is paved with joy, not with targets and numerical standards". His advice – "Seek joy, and success will naturally follow".

Love your work

Only one life to live. Do whatever you want to do. Love and enjoy what you do. Listen to the messages from wise people:

"It is not doing the thing we like, it is liking the thing we have to do that makes life happy."
Immanuel Kant, British philosopher

"The true way to render ourselves happy is to love our work and find in it pleasure."
Francoise de Motteville, French author

"Love your work. If you always put your heart into every thing you do, you really can't lose. Whether you wind up making a lot of money or not, you will have had a wonderful time, and no one will ever be able to take that away from you."
Alan Alda, American author

"To love what you do and feel that it matters—how could anything be more fun."
Catherine Graham, American poet

"Success is not the key to happiness. Happiness is the key to success. If you love what you are doing you will be successful."
Herman Cain, Inspiring speaker

Find joy in your work

Look at the job offers. Every employer describes the vacant position and offers some salary and other benefits. Eligible aspirants apply and join the work. Sooner or later many people look for greener pastures elsewhere, no matter how distant. Higher emoluments, of course, do attract many. But what baffles one is that even those in higher brackets seek a change. Are they struck by ennui to search for alternative? Most probably, you are right. The simple reason is that work is not about salary or money, it is more about satisfaction. The subtle secret is that they expect that work should provide opportunities to fulfill all their aspirations—social and emotional. But unfortunately work cannot provide everything they are looking for. "Many people think that if they were only in some other place, or had some other job they would be happy," points out Success guru Dale Carnegie. "Well, that is doubtful. So, get as much happiness out of what you are doing as you can and don't put off being happy until some future date."

Such people suffer from a dangerous attitude that "everything in life is some where else." Why should they go any where else? Many people who are not happy with positional power that comes with the job, look for personal power elsewhere. We often see such people eagerly wanting to be 'chairman' or 'secretary' or 'treasurer' of an association outside their work. Those who feel that work is monotonous and boring, seek joy in recreational activities—sports, painting, music, acting, dancing, etc. within or outside the ambit of work. Some others indulge in their favourite hobbies.

They do not realise that joy is not located in work. Joy comes from inside. One should look within for what they really want. We are probably conditioned in our upbringing what to look for in work. Joy comes from the way we feel while engaged in work or while doing anything. Work can only serve as a catalyst that allows us to feel the joy.

"Work is yet another resource as well as great therapy, an anodyne against pain," says American writer Ardis Whitman. "The more difficult and challenging the thing we are working at, the better, for we can't work hard without using up some of the energy that might go into self-pity." The more creative attitude towards work, the greater enrichment we can draw from it.

"Happiness: She loves to see men at work," says American journalist David Grayson. "She loves sweat, weariness, sacrifice. She will be found not in palaces but lurking in fields and factories, hovering over littered desks. She crowns the unconscious head of the busy child."

"There is joy in work. All that money can do is buy us someone else's work in exchange for our own. There is no happiness except in the realisation that we accomplished something," says American Industrialist Henry Ford. "Work joyfully, and peacefully, knowing that right thoughts and right efforts will inevitably bring about the right results," says American writer James Lane Allen. Yes, get happiness out of your work or you may never know what happiness is.

Work and play

"For adults the most satisfying hours of life are those spent in interesting and absorbing, exciting work," says Nobel laureate Pearl S. Buck. "What such work provides is provided to children in play, stretching their capacity to enjoy, perform to achieve." Yes, we learn from the very childhood that there is joy in playing with things; and we continue to enjoy playful work. "There is work that is work and there is play that is play; there is play that is work and work that is play. And in only one of these lies happiness," says American humorist Gilett Burgess. "You know you have achieved success in your own field when you don't know what you are doing is work or play," says Hollywood actor Warren Beaty. We spend more time working than any other activity. We often forget that work can become play—a source of joy. You will gain more pleasure from playful work.

Discover the joyful 'flow'

"Whenever we are involved in activities that are rewarding in and of themselves, a joyful feeling—"flow"—emerges", says psychologist Mihaly Csikszentmihalyi (hereafter Dr. C). "It develops when we are completely immersed in what we are doing and lose a sense of self and time. In this state, a person gains a heightened awareness of his physical involvement with activity, and his enjoyment is enormously enhanced." He believes, this feeling of flow is the "fun" in fun. According to him the real enjoyment comes from 'flow'—the ecstatic feeling of total immersion in what we are doing.

Dr. C found that the extrinsic rewards are less stimulating to the spirit than the intrinsic pleasure of the "flow." He says that some people devote a great deal of energy to activities that do not return any extrinsic rewards; their real reward—was flow, an altered state of being that occurred when people were enjoying their activity most. Read what he says about flow in work:

- People in *flow* undergo an intense centring of attention on the activity. Though they do not *try* to concentrate harder, concentration comes automatically.
- In *flow*, the individual experiences an altered sense of time. "Time passes a hundred times faster. In this sense it resembles the dream state," says one chess player.
- Sometimes the centring of attention produces a spatial alteration. In his prime, golfer Arnold Palmer could look at a putt and see a line on the green from ball to cup.
- There is no sense of self. A tennis player in *flow* is not bothered by such thoughts as "Am I doing well?" If the moment is split so that the player perceives his action from outside, then flow halts.
- Another factor is the clarity of response that the individual gets from the activity—the internal sense of rightness. But

the person in *flow* does not stop to evaluate this sense. He is too involved with the experience to reflect upon it.
- *Flow* can make a person feel an almost godlike sense of control. All of life's conflicts seem resolved.

According to Dr. C, to induce *flow*, an activity must allow an individual to meet a challenge at the outer limits of his capability without testing him *beyond* those limits. If an activity is too simple, he is bored. But if the test is too severe, he begins worrying about its severity, and about himself. Anxiety stops the flow. To facilitate a centring of attention, suggests Dr. C, the activity should have a ritual preceding it.

A surprisingly diverse number of activities have the potential of producing flow. It can help improve our attitude towards work. Putting more emphasis on the intrinsic quality of the work itself could put flow back into work and thus enrich your life. The sense of joy that comes from work can transform a life of stress and strain into a life of sweetness and comfort. US novelist Willa Sibert Cather says, "That is happiness: to be dissolved into something complete and great." You must lose yourself in what you like as it fills your heart with joyful flow.

Find joy in your relationships at the workplace

Joy of work is not confined to your work alone. Joy also comes from workplace where your boss and colleagues appreciate your skills, admire your workmanship, and recognise you as a valuable colleague. Create a good image and establish rapport with all people who work with you. Improve your visibility as a good worker. Create and nurture healthy relationships with every person in the organisation. Remember people smell rat the moment they sense manipulation or manoeuvering. Honesty and trustworthiness pay everywhere. Never forget to enjoy the company of your colleagues.

Enjoy work, take sufficient rest

You are justified in getting immersed in work because it is one of the chief sources of joy and happiness in life. But remember, demanding gut-busting performance from yourself can put you on the edge. A break from hard work will certainly refresh the mind and body. Getting a few moments of respite over the course of work can save you from possible breakdown. Step out and get some fresh air. A couple of deep breathes in between any task can help ease your pace. It has a relaxing and rejuvenating effect on your body. Stretch your back, neck and the leg muscles and relax for a while. A relaxed body is less prone to health problems. Forget what you were doing for a few minutes. Shift your focus from the restless activities of the day to a more peaceful state of mind. Think of the joy of doing whatever you like. Dedicate a few moments for yourself and think of the joy of living.

Work and family life

Fluid lines overlap between work and personal space. We often take our personalities to work, while work related thoughts influence our family life. It is always better to forget work while at home. Working for long hours is known to have a telling effect on family life. It has been confirmed in a recent study by Working Families, a Charity Organisation in London. Its chief executive Sarah Jackson says, "This disturbing report shows us that binge-working is turning us into a nation of workaholics. This is having disastrous effect on our health, our family life and our performance at work... The impact on their health could be seen in increased irritability (48 per cent), sleeplessness (44 per cent), lack of exercise (36per cent), and exhaustion (35 per cent)."

You need to relax more after work. Unwind totally when you get back home. A few physical exercises can have a moderating influence on bodily tensions. Exercise is a great stress buster, it can calm down your agitating emotions. You may try some more relaxing methods like body massage. See how refreshed you are after a hot-water bath.

Pursue some leisure time activities, if you can. Hobbies like reading, painting, stitching and embroidery, gardening, watching TV programmes, etc. can drain away the mental stress, if any. Happiness may be as close as your garden. Have a variety of interests, they relax the mind and lessen the strain on the nervous system. It is believed that people with many interests not only live longest but the happiest. Once in a while plan a holiday. Just get away from work routine and do something you enjoy.

Sharing life with your family members is important to ensure a joyful life. Think of any activity or a home project that allows you to take part with your loved ones. Spend some pleasurable moments with your children and discover the joy of being a parent. Playing with them, helping them to learn, proper upbringing are the most satisfying activities. Share intimate moments with your spouse and experience the bliss of family life and the joy of living. Get sufficient sleep during night, so that you wake up refreshed ready to do a day's job tomorrow. Yes, as philosopher Albert Einstein says, "you are justified in looking to the future with true assurance, because you have a mode of living in which joy of living and joy of work are harmoniously combined."

Seek fulfillment in a noble cause

People walk different roads seeking fulfillment and happiness. You are welcome to choose your own way. "Are you bored in life?" asks Personal Development Guru Dale Carnegie. "Then throw yourself into some work you believe in with all your heart, live for it, die for it, you will find happiness that you had thought could never be yours." Scientist Jack H Gosling also pleads on the same lines: "If you would find happiness and joy, lose your life in a noble cause. A worthy purpose must be at the centre of a worthy life."

Satisfy Your Needs: Enjoy What You Get

> The secret of contentment is knowing how to enjoy what you have, and be able to lose desire for things beyond reach.
>
> *Lin Yutang (1895-1916)*
> Chinese-American writer

> To be without some of the things you want is an indispensable part of happiness.
>
> *Bertrand Russell (1872-1970)*
> British Mathematician and Philosopher
> Nobel prize for literature 1950

Man tries to get anything he wants

When a person desires anything in life, he will try to get it by any means—by hook or crook. Satisfaction of his needs and desires is the primary objective, and the happiness that follows is the ultimate goal. It doesn't matter if he has to compromise his values. Sometimes he is even prepared to transgress the norms of society or break laws of the land, to get what he wants. That is the power of man's desires that drive him to do anything. Examine your needs and desires and find what really you want in life.

Basic needs are limited

"What we call happiness in the strictest sense comes from (preferably sudden) satisfaction of needs which have been damned up to a higher degree," says Sigmund Freud, an Austrian psychiatrist.

Psychologist Abraham Maslow identifies a hierarchy of needs:

Physical needs: food and thirst, sleep, health, body needs, exercise, rest and sex.

Safety needs: security and safety, protection, comfort, and peace, no threats or danger, orderly and neat surroundings.

Social needs: Acceptance, feeling of belonging, membership in a group, love and affection, and group participation.

Self-esteem needs: recognition and prestige, confidence and leadership, achievement and ability, competence and success, strength and intelligence.

Self-actualisation: Self-fulfillment of potential, doing things purely for the challenge of accomplishment, intellectual curiosity and fulfilment, creativity and aesthetic appreciation, acceptance of reality, and transcendence (the need to help others in their self-fulfillment to realise their potential). During his last days Maslow also recognised the need for happiness and peace.

Psychologists have found other needs. The need for achievement is the need to succeed and strive against the standards of excellence; it serves to motivate an individual to do well. The need for power is the need to influence the behaviour of others. The need for affiliation is the need to associate with people.

We learn from our very childhood that food and shelter are necessary for our survival. After hunger and thirst, sex is our strongest need. As pointed by H. Jackson Brown, "Intimacy can be compared to food and shelter, because we need it as much. But just as with food and shelter, no one needs it all the time, and some people need it more than others." Most people agree that nothing comes close to sexual ecstasy; yet it isn't everything in life.

Romantic sex is different from sex for sale. Romantic sex generally leads to family life. Whereas sex for sale relates to the unethical practice of sleeping with anyone for money. In any case over-indulgence may lead to health problems, if not venereal diseases like AIDS.

Drinking, dining, dancing, and enjoying sex are pleasurable activities. They not only satisfy our needs but contribute to our happiness. Life without these pleasures is indeed miserable. But over-indulgence is certainly not desirable. In this context listen to Jewish philosopher Baruch Spinoza : "Indulge yourself in pleasures only in so far as they are necessary for preservation of health."

Compared to other needs the self-actualisation needs are the most neglected. Unless we discover and use them, they go waste. Martin EP Seligman of Pennsylvania University says, "Realise your potential abilities for lasting fulfillment. They are the source of enduring happiness."

Acquired needs are unlimited

Wants that satisfy basic needs are necessities; whereas the wants that satisfy our desires are luxuries. They constitute ego satisfying wants. Most of the people would like to enjoy these luxuries; and they are prepared to do anything to acquire them. We may call this desire for these things as acquired needs.

Unlimited wants and limited resources: that's the problem

We would like to indulge in many expensive things, over and above the ordinary necessities of life, to enjoy, amuse, and entertain ourselves. These are often called luxuries which gratify our appetites and tastes—such as rich food, costly dress, luxurious mansions, expensive cars, etc. We want to possess all the ego-satisfying things that our money can buy.

Things we don't really need but badly want are unlimited wants. As long as basic needs are met these unlimited luxuries charm the rich as well as the poor. Many people spend a lot of money on what they don't need but what they desire. As philosopher Eric Hoffer says, "You can never get enough of what you don't need to make you happy." This is where misplaced priorities dominate man's actions that spoil all the fun in life. English author Oliver Goldsmith says, "If frugality were established in the state, and if our expenses are laid out to meet the needs rather than superficialities of life, there might be fewer wants, even fewer pleasures, but infinitely more happiness." Roman philosopher Marcus Aurelius Antoninus goes one step ahead, "Very little is needed to make a happy life."

No end to the problem until we limit our desires

Many wise people have advocated the wisdom of limiting human desires. Let us consider some of them:

"May we never let the things we can't have, don't have or shouldn't have, spoil our enjoyment of the things we do have and can have. As we value our happiness let us not forget, for one of the greatest lessons in life is learning to be happy without the things we cannot or should not have."
Richard L. Evans, American writer

"Civilisation in the real sense of the term, consists not in the multiplication, but in the deliberate and voluntary restriction of wants."
Mahatma Gandhi

"I have learned to seek happiness by limiting my desires, rather than attempting to satisfy them."
John Stuart Mill, British philosopher

"To be without some of the things you want is an indispensable part of happiness."

Bertrand Russell, British philosopher

"Perfection of wisdom and the end of true philosophies is to proportion our wants to our possessions, our ambitions to our capacities. We will be then happy and virtuous people."

Mark Twain, American author

"There are two ways of being happy. We must either diminish our wants or augment our means—either may do—the result is same; and it is for each man to decide for himself and to do that which happens to be easier."

Benjamin Franklin, American Statesman

Money has now become the supreme need

Whether or not money is humanity's greatest invention, its meanings reveal a great deal about human nature. "Money is a frozen desire," says economist James Buchan in *Frozen Desire: The Meaning of Money*. He says, " Men and women chase money as energetically as they chase each other. Because money can fulfill any mortal purpose, for many people the pursuit of money becomes the point of life." Undoubtedly money today has become the supreme need of mankind superseding all other needs. Almost everybody is eager to acquire and accumulate wealth.

The recent concern for money the world over is perhaps unprecedented. Everybody is showing a lot of enthusiasm for aggressive pursuit of money. People are taking greater risks to acquire wealth. Never before has the world witnessed such a phenomenon. It has now become an epidemic.

The urgent need to create wealth is causing agony and misery to many people. Recently the advertising giant, Lowe and Partners, conducted a research survey about how people feel about making money, in five Asian cities – Hong Kong, Singapore, Shanghai, Bangkok and Jakarta. It has been reported that the people in Hong Kong are the most stressed because of the pressure to make money quickly. This phenomenon is not confined to Asian countries, it is spread all over the world. But they don't realise that they need not kill themselves to be financially successful.

Money is necessary to buy what we want
Money has exchange value. We need it to buy things required for survival. It is absolutely necessary to buy goods and services that satisfy our needs. Because of this reason man has developed a tendency to acquire money. Many people openly express disdain for money, as if it is possible to live on this earth without money. "It is a spiritual snobbery that makes people think they can be happy without money," says Nobel laureate Albert Camus.

Money plays an important role in our social life. Modern living has become so superficial that it gives more importance to riches and material things than human values. Money matters more than breeding, faith and monarchy. It is being treated as the basic constituent and the fundamental element in life. It is associated with riches, properties, and all the material things that money can buy.

Many things in life are not necessary for survival. Yet we like to acquire them to satisfy our egoistic desires. We usually experience extreme pleasure when we acquire highly expensive things like diamonds, luxury cars, or stately mansions, etc. Such things may increase our hedonic response—a process that economists call *satisfaction*. On the other hand, when we lose these glitzy things we experience agony and anguish.

Even if we experience extreme pleasure immediately after acquisition of most desired things, we tend to revert back to stable levels of well-being—that is, to the initial level of happiness. That is what Economists Brick and Campbell call 'hedonistic treadmill.' In other words they explain that the happiness derived from such conspicuous goods is short-lived.

No amount of money can increase happiness or ease the sorrow

"It is pretty hard to tell what does bring happiness, poverty or wealth have both failed," observes American Cartoonist Journalist Kin Hubbard. "Money never made a man happy yet, nor will it," says American Statesman Benjamin Franklin. "There is nothing in its nature to produce happiness. The more a man has, the more he wants. Instead of its filling the vacuum, it makes one." Philanthropist Sir John Templeton says, " Happiness comes from spiritual wealth, not material wealth. Happiness comes from giving not getting."

According to the comic genius Spike Milligan, "Money can't buy you happiness, but it does bring a more pleasant form of misery." Finally listen to Irish writer J P Donleavy: "When you don't have money, the problem is food. When you have money, it's sex. When you have both it's health. If everything is simple Jake, then you are frightened of death." No amount of money can increase happiness nor ease sorrow.

Habit of accumulating money is universal

People may express general disdain for money, but in heart of hearts they are after it. Income expansion matters, especially to the poor; it enables them to gain access to goods and services. People think that higher income will help realise their dreams. They try to make more money and accumulate as much as they can.

"There is nothing so habit forming as money," says American author Don Marquis. We continue the habit of acquiring and accumulating more money, even after our needs have been satisfied. This is what psychologists call 'functional fixedness'. But any amount of money does not guarantee what people cherish and value: happiness. If we can be happy with what we have, we won't desire more money. If we are enjoying what we have, we always have enough money to be happy.

Don't be obsessed with money

When you treat money as an end rather than means, it becomes a magnificent obsession. It neither satisfies all the needs nor guarantees happiness. Here it would be nice to know the mind of wise people about the obsession with money:

> "Money is human happiness in the abstract: he, then, who is no longer capable of enjoying human happiness in the concrete devotes his heart entirely to money."
> *Arthur Schopenhauer, German philosopher*

> "If you love money you will never be satisfied. If you long to be rich you will never get all you want."
> *Solomon, Wise King of Ancient Israel*

> "If money is all that one makes, then he will be poor—poor in happiness, poor in all that makes life worth living."
> *Herbert N Casson, American Journalist*

> "Prosperity is living easily and happily in the real world, whether you have money or not."
> *Jerry Gellis, American author*

> "It is better to lose a billion dollars than a good night's sleep."
> *N.R.Narayanamurthy, Founder of Infosys Technologies*

Money and personal worth

Money may give some status in society. But you must remember that it cannot increase your personal worth. Your value as a person does not change, no matter how rich you are. A person who has the mistaken notion that money can enhance his personal worth often inflates his ego when he acquires a lot of money; but he becomes a punctured tube when he loses money. Therefore, it is always better to keep your ego far from money; though you require it for your sustenance.

Money and morals
Whether it is business or work, sports or service, whatever it is making money is also part of the motivation. Pursuit of wealth and fulfilment of desires should only be within the ambit of our morals. According to Mahatma Gandhi, "Wealth without character and business without morality are self-destructive."

Learn to manage your money
You must always keep an eye on your money. Find out where your money is and where it goes. Protect what you have, otherwise the moment you open your palm, money will run away fast like a centipede.

Anyone who does not know how to manage money is doomed to have financial problems in life. You must include financial planning as part of your life-planning. List your dreams and future goals, quantify them in monetary terms, and then work backward to see if they are achievable, given your resources.

"A household is really a business," reminds Diane Kennedy, an expert on finance. "Track your personal expenses and business expenses," is her simple practical advice.

- *Increase your resources or reduce your expenditure.* Be aware of your money needs and try to balance your income with expenditure. Your spending pattern will reveal your style of living. Therefore it is good to check up and know how you are spending money. It will give you an insight into your priorities in life. Examine why you are always short of money. You may have to reduce your expenditure or increase your income. If you don't cut avoidable expenditure, you may find it difficult to find when you badly need it.
- *Keep limited cash on hand.* You need some money for near term transactions. Never keep more cash than you need. Have a small amount with you; it is not safe to keep more money at home either. Keep some ready money in a bank so that

you can draw whenever you are in need. It is better to use a debit card than a credit card.
- *Don't buy what you don't need.* Don't be a compulsive buyer. Buy what you need for survival and buy what you can without borrowing. Heed the warning of former American President Thomas Jefferson: " Never buy what you don't want because it is cheap; it will be dear (costly) to you."
- *Budget your money for daily needs.* Provisions, food items, daily services, need careful allocation. Budgeting is necessary, especially when prices are rising. Check how you are making, and allocating money for various needs. Learn to budget your income and spend it wisely. If you don't balance your income with your expenditure it will create endless emotional problems.
- *Think of short-term expenditure.* You need money for pilgrimages, holidays, tours, picnics, social occasions. Consider your short-term money requirements. If you don't have money you don't have to commit heavy expenditure.
- *Save for long-term money needs.* Keep your values, dreams and goals in mind while providing money for future. A dream house, a small car, children's education, their marriages, retirement are always on the agenda. Plan and save money needed for long-term requirements. Keep some family welfare fund. Think of savings, bank deposits, insurance or some investments. "Save today smile tomorrow" they say. But if you save, one thing is sure, you will not weep. Those who do not take care of this responsibility will suffer when the need arises. You can learn a lesson from the suffering retired people who neglected their responsibilities.
- *Provide for emergencies.* Events like accidents, disability, unemployment, crises, diseases and death knock us down without notice. They don't give us enough time to recover.

But we can absorb the shocks if we keep a soft cushion of money. You never know when you need large sums of money. Always keep sufficient money in the bank as an emergency fund to meet unexpected expenses. Otherwise you may have to borrow or suffer. If you get any windfall money keep it aside to meet unexpected emergencies.

Make sure you have not lost what money can't buy
Thoughts of money occupy our mind all the time because money is required for comfortable living. Keep a track of money in and out of your life. At the same time be aware that money can't buy happiness; it can only buy material things. You must learn to keep a healthy distance from money, if you want to be happy. "It is good to have money and the things that money can buy, but it is good to check up once in a while to make sure you haven't lost the things that money can't buy," says an American Clergyman George Claude Lorimer.

Enjoy what you have: get instant happiness
Success is in getting what you want, and happiness is in liking what you get. As American writer Frederick Koenig says, "We tend to forget that happiness does not come as result of getting something we don't have, but rather of recognising and appreciating what we do have." Happiness only comes from appreciating what you have right now. If you think that something will make you happy, strive to get it by any means, though you are not sure about the result. American business philosopher Jim Rohn says, "Learn how to be happy with what you have, and pursue all that you want." Yes, you can be happy when you get what you want; but why postpone enjoying what you have. As Clergyman Charles Spurgeon says, "It is not how much we have, but how much we enjoy, that makes happiness."

"There are two things to aim in life," says American author Logan Pearsal. "First get what you want; and after that to enjoy it. The wisest of the mankind achieve the second." Think that you have succeeded in life when all you really want is what you really get. If you want instant happiness don't search for it anywhere else: *enjoy what you have* before you look for what you desire! Remember, it isn't what you have that makes you happy, but what you enjoy!

Realise Dreams, Achieve Goals: Don't Forget to Enjoy the Endeavour

What you can do or dream you can, begin it. Boldness has genius, power and magic in it.

Johann Wolfgang von Goethe (1749-1832)
German poet, novelist, playwright, natural philosopher

If you want to have a happy life, tie it to a goal, not to people or things.

Albert Einstein (1879-1955)
Philosopher, physicist
Nobel Prize for physics 1921.

Joy of Dreaming is Universal
" We would still be in dark ages were it not for wishful thinking. Without it most of the achievements of mankind would never have been started," points out Psychologist Alex F. Osborn, author of *Applied Imagination*. Yes, dreams are necessary to mankind, as they pave the way to achievement and progress in the world.

The creative genius of mind weaves magic around our fantasies and wishes, needs and wants, problems and crises, hopes and fears, and everything required in our lives. As it is a universal phenomenon, everyone gets endless dreams that give unlimited delight. "Day-dreams are normal to all active minds. They make our lives more creative and original," says Professor Jerome Singer of Yale University (*Reader's Digest*, Oct. '76).

Our dreams and goals are dear to us. We love our dreams because they are the reflections of our hopes and fears, ambitions and aspirations and all that we want in life. Like pathfinders they always go ahead throwing light on our life-path. The most endearing charm of dreams is their possibility to become a joyful reality. " Dreams are renewable. No matter our age or condition, there are still untapped possibilities within us and new beauty is waiting to be born," says American author Mark Twain. They have mesmeric effect on our lives always inspiring exciting possibilities. That is what fascinates human beings; they nurture the delightful feeling that everything is possible in life. They keep goading us till we achieve what we want in life. In fact, they help us find new directions in life. "Our dreams and visions are imaginary, yet they have tremendous impact on our lives. A lot of good things have come out of dreaming," says American playwright Arthur Miller. Perhaps that is the reason why Lebanese philosopher Kahlil Gibran exhorts: "Trust the dreams, for in them is hidden the gates of eternity."

Dream big, dare to pursue higher goals

For young people owning a fast bike or sports car can be a dream. Standing first in the class can be another dream. Getting into a lucrative job can be another dream. Marrying a beautiful girl or handsome man can still be another dream. Making lots of money may be the ultimate dream. People keep dreaming all the while, day and night, about things in life they wish to enjoy.

Most people who come from not so rich families know how difficult it is to survive in this world. Many people struggle a lot to live a decent life. We experience the daily grind of life, endless family chores, education of children, care of infants and invalids, unemployment or under employment, insufficient income, unsatisfied needs, marriage and social obligations, occasional health problems, recurring money troubles and many untold hardships. Because our real life is hard, it is natural for us to dream of a better life in future. But we all know how difficult it is to realise even smaller dreams. This does not however discourage us from dreaming what we wish to enjoy in life. "Cherish your visions and dreams as they are children of your soul, the blue prints of your achievements," says success guru Napoleon Hill. "Whatever your mind can conceive and believe, it can achieve."

Dreams remain unfulfilled due to lack of confidence, negative thinking, improper planning, lack of commitment or the needed efforts. Never underestimate the value of your dream. It may look outlandish to others, but it is so dear to you because it is your own. Dream what you wish and throw your dream into space like a kite and watch what it may bring back—a new life, a new friend, a new love. Sky is the limit. Millionaire Billy Idol says," If your world doesn't allow you to dream, move to one where you can."

Visualise before realising your dream

Your happiness is just a dream away. Your dream is actually the reality in waiting. You can imagine and visualise your dream before you realise it. Imaginative visualisation is another way of enjoying the dream. Visualisation is like living your dream for a few moments and seeing how things really look when realised. An experiment conducted by Alan Richardson, an Australian psychologist, found 23% improvement in the performance of his subjects who visualised (their dream projects) every day for 20 days. Richardson wrote, "the most effective visualisation occurs when the subject feels and sees what he is doing."

The ability to achieve is a pre-requirement to realise your dream. Orville Wright and Wilbur Wright were no doubt inspired by Leonardo da Vinci's designs of flying machines. Obviously, that inspiration in itself was not enough to drive them to action. It was the wonderful phenomenon of visualisation followed by executive action that resulted in practical experiments. They saw in their minds how various forms of flying machines look, and how they could carry men and materials. After years of experiments, learning from trial and error, they did realise their dream on December 17, 1903.

Even as I write this, the media flashed a news item on 23 March 2005, from London *Telegraph*. It is about a British teenager Martin Halstead who realised his dream of becoming a pilot. He opened his own Alpha 1 Airways that will operate between Oxford and Cambridge. Take a look at his dream and admire his determination to realise it: "Flying was my passion since I was six. I have never wanted anything other than to be a pilot, but I did," and he is reported to have said, "To my surprise I was offered the chance to start almost straight away. Such was my desire to become a pilot that I was given the backing of my parents and my principal to leave the school without completing my A-levels."

Visualisation is seeing the future destination of your dream in advance—every step of your actions before you realise the dream. That will pave the way for inspired action and exciting results. Both visualisation of dream and its realisation offer unlimited joy. So, learn to visualise how your dream looks like when realised. Mike Yates, the management guru, reminds us Genghis Khan's formula for success: *envision, enable, empower, energise*. Yes, you require all these.

Nurture and nourish your dream

Don't forget to nurture your dream. Like a child a dream has to be taken by the lapel and told, "I am with you kid, let's go." Like a parent, you must look after and nourish your dream till such time it gathers strength to stand on its own. But then, you should know what nutrients are needed to make it grow into an adult—your dream-project. Dreams delight us for a while; but dream-projects go one step ahead: they throb us with lasting joy for a life time.

Magic of commitment

Have you ever wondered how Shah Jahan realised his dream project of Taj Mahal, a marvellous memorial for his beloved queen Mumtaj Mahal? It was indeed a symbol of love and commitment. Imagine the pooled talents of architects from all over the world, the indefatigable zeal and undeterred perseverance of native builders, sustained effort of thousands of workers who toiled for years. Your dream-project, say a house of your own, may not be on such a grand scale; nevertheless it requires the same kind of ingredients: money and materials, talent and skills, patience and persistence, time and effort. It needs solid commitment, diligent preparation, and tenacious effort. When you nurture your dream with these nutrients, they empower your dream to become a reality. Therefore you have to strengthen your natural talents and abilities and streamline your efforts.

Commit to your dream and give your best till you realise it. That is the only secret to ensure success in life. When you dedicate yourself to your dream, it may seem like an obsession to the onlookers. Tell them it is your commitment in disguise. Align your dream with your strong self-image to counter any doubts that may arise. Once you reinforce yourself with sufficient confidence in your skills and abilities, nothing can sabotage your dream. When you put these wings on your dream, you can be rest assured that your dream can take the next flight to the real world.

Inspired action is the key

"A vision without the ability to execute is probably a hallucination," points out Stephen M Case, the co-founder of America On Line. Yes, visualisation without action is merely an enlarged dream. Most of us enjoy the joy ride on the magic carpet of dreams. Just thinking how wonderful is the dream, takes you no where. Unless you follow it up with determination, and commitment it remains a mirage. To realise dreams you need inspired action that springs from within, unlike the forced action that comes from without. Inspired action is joyful action that is in alignment with your dream. When you are inspired to do something, you are committed to completing it and things automatically fall in place to make your dream come true.

Some times inspiration can come from people who have realised their dreams. Be in touch with such experienced people to get inspired. They can be your guides if not role models. Take their help and guidance whenever you need. You can learn a lot from their experience. Know what they have learnt from their mistakes, so it will help you avoid similar mistakes.

Explore the realm of possibilities

Dreams in general are wishful fantasies like myths; but unlike myths they can become real by the efforts of the dreamer (you). "Dreams come true," assures a well-known American author John Updike, "Without that possibility nature would not incite us to have them." So, don't entertain any doubts about the possibility of realising your dream. What all you have to do is to ensure that your dream is realistic, so that it has a fair chance of becoming true.

In a word, explore possibilities—you will find they are as varied as your wit and imagination. This is important because no one can realise a dream if it is beyond the realm of possibility. If you want your dream to become true the first requirement is, you must ensure its realistic possibility.

Increase the probabilities

Work out various ways to make the dream project probable. It is not enough if a thing is possible. Possibility is one thing and the likelihood of success is another. Unless success is probable we can't achieve anything. That is why we must hold back a bit to determine the chances of success before devoting our full energy to the project. To increase the probability of success of any dream project we have to ensure that it is feasible. "It is best to act when feasible, if not see what is possible," advises an ancient Pallava Raj Guru Thiru Valluvar. To be successful, you must study the feasibility of your dream project. Besides feasibility, we have to take into account the required resources—men, materials and skills and expertise, time, effort, etc. Above all, what matters is your determination to achieve and the expected satisfaction. That is what increases the probability of success. Only then it can become true.

Just do it: don't tell others

Just do it, the way you want! When you share your dreams with others you run the risk of taking your plans to the oblivion. Others can be sceptical for one thousand reasons. Sometimes it is simple jealousy. They will never be as enthusiastic as you are. Their lack of enthusiasm may be enough to kill your desire to pursue what may have been a fantastic opportunity. After you have realised your dream you will have plenty of time to talk about it, but you will be too busy having fun.

Have an action plan

Planning is vital for any achievement, because 'failing to plan is planning to fail'. Life-plan approach is necessary to achieve success in life. It should include your needs, dreams and goals. If you really want to realise your dream you have to come down to earth from the world of fantasies. Sit up and get down to work. The first and foremost thing is to examine the possibility and feasibility of your dream project. Examine whether you can do it with or without outside help. Remember, real men don't ask for help, unless it is absolutely necessary. If you think you can do it, the next thing to do is to arrive at a plan of action within the framework of your present needs and future goals. Remember, unimplemented plans don't mean anything. " If you go to work on goals, your goals will go to work for you," says Jim Rohn, the American business philosopher. "If you go to work on your plan, your plan will go to work for you. Whatever good things we build we end up building us."

Planning is meaningful if it is propelled by the deep desire to realise the dream. It can be successful if it meets the requirements of the need to achieve. Diligent planning of your dream project is necessary because it gives some control over the turn of events. It gives a measure of progress as you proceed. It should take into account your abilities and resources. Never forget your family responsibilities. Another important thing is to balance your life-goals with your duties and moral obligations.

Never plan for distant future because it is uncertain. Think of immediate term and think of what is possible to achieve and reasonably predictable. What to do and when to do depends on your decisions. When in doubt trust your instincts. But never forget to take responsibility for the consequences of your actions.

If you can chalk out a dream-plan with the action-steps, you can jump into action any time. Start with what you are good at, for it will have a better chance of becoming a success. Find your own rhythm and pursue every step in a measured manner at your own pace. Surely, you will enjoy every moment of it.

Work out action steps

In order to implement your plan strategies, you may have to break down your plan into action steps that can be done one at a time. Keep them simple so that you can handle them with greater ease. Then visualise the end result of each step and see how it fits into the overall plan and then move on. Surely, you will encounter real life problems while implementing your action steps. It is here you need greater flexibility and faster adaptability.

Set a time-frame

"For happy people the time is filled and planned," says psychologist Michel Argyle. "For unhappy people time is unfilled. They postpone things and are inefficient," You must have a reasonable time-frame for your dream project. Break down action steps into separate small manageable tasks with a definite time schedule. If you set deadlines of your own you may probably ignore them. But if you give deadlines in the presence of someone close to you, a friend or spouse, you will have to save your face when you don't meet your commitment. Your pride will make you finish the job in time.

Think of priorities

Setting priorities is an antidote for overload of work. It can reduce a lot of wasteful time. "The essence of best thinking in the area of time management may be captured by a single phrase: Organise and execute around priorities," says psychologist Stephen R. Covey. According to him the best self-manager is one who executes tasks according to their importance rather than urgency. Therefore, think of 'first things first' while executing your project. That is what we mean by priorities. Decide on the importance of each task first and set priorities. Don't waste time on trivial things however urgent they may look. Take up the most important task first with full force and effort. Once it is completed, think of other priorities and take up tasks depending on their importance.

And soon you will see the Zeigarnik effect—other uncompleted tasks will pull your attention to complete them.

Find the required resources
Do the homework and find the resources, before you try to realise your dream. Yes, without means you can't achieve anything. Therefore think of all the things that are required to make your dream come true— resources like money and time, men and material, equipment and methods, contacts and help, everything that is required. It has been said that 'true happiness is born of self-reliance.' " To survive in the 21st century you need to depend on your yourself—your labour, your knowledge, and your entrepreneurial spirit," says American writer Larry C. Farrel in *Getting Entrepreneurial*. It is easier to accomplish when you align your dream with your own talents, skills, courage, determination and effort.

Provide for contingencies
Many events have a knack of happening without prior notice. You never know what additional problems you are likely to encounter. Remember, no problem is strong enough to strike you down, though it can disappoint you. Never think of giving up. Think of eventualities that may occur and foresee the possible ways you can deal with them. Prepare in advance to meet those contingencies. To save yourself from unexpected onslaughts, always keep aside some resources. That will ensure your resilience, 'to be the last man standing.'

Jump start with what you have
Attempting anything with what you are good at, requires far less time and effort to achieve success. When it comes to realising dreams, the best thing to do is to start with what we have. "Do what you can, with what you have, where you are," advises former US President Theodore Roosevelt." You don't have to wait for

anything, anyone, or any situation before you make a positive change in your life," says American author Marilyn Tam in *How to Use What You Have to Get What You Want.*

A common excuse is to say you would do once you know it. "Learn it on the run," exhorts Tam. "And once you get into something, do it one hundred per cent; this does not involve 'life and limb' but just that you've to be fully present and dedicated in the project you have embarked on." Another important thing is to start small. It is easy to be successful with small projects; and they will surely boost up your self-confidence.

"Use what works for you," advises Robert Sheinfeld in *The Invisible Path to Success.* "This works for everything, be it nutrition, exercise, how to run your business, and how to invest your money. He says, " if you are motivated enough go ahead and try it. If it works for you, use it. If it doesn't, keep looking until you find something that does work for you." According to him, the key is " through experience," not thought.

Doing it yourself is okay, but not advisable as a long-term strategy. Remember, very few can achieve goals without other's help. Look for people who are interested in you and willing to help—mentors, parents, siblings, relatives and friends. Surely you can benefit from their help. There is nothing wrong in looking up for help from people who have 'been there' and done that. Learning from such people can help you gain the required skills rapidly. Try to synergise your efforts with what they can offer—experience, skills, talents, cooperation, contacts, and money. They can provide the right support, though free advice sometimes hinders progress. Many of them are generally helpful, but there is no guarantee that you will get all you ask for. You will definitely be benefited by making an earnest effort. On the other hand, this may help you to know who your true friends are.

Streamline your efforts
"No great thing is created suddenly any more than a bunch of grapes or a fig," says Epictetus. Nothing can be achieved without effort; remember even performing below par needs effort. "Streamline your efforts and strengthen your natural talent and ability through education and experience," advises Stacey Mayo, founder of Centre for Balanced Living. This is important because your dream project needs relentless effort to realise it. Focus on one project at a time. If you try to do several things at a time, your efforts are likely to be wasted without proper use. Remember, scattered efforts often result in poor outcomes. Concerted actions and unflagging efforts are like milk and honey that nurture your dream-project to become a reality.

Evaluate periodically, and review progress
Follow up is one of the essential steps in most of the planned projects. It has to be done periodically with a view to checking the progress towards the goals. Your life-plan may look perfect, but you will know what it is lacking or what more is needed. Your plans may have been well-drafted, but things always have a knack of going astray like the unleashed dogs. Being the owner of the plan, you have to watch every step while implementing it. Check periodically whether it is on the right track and as per the schedule. Check what didn't work and where things went wrong. Examine what corrective steps need to be taken.

Be prepared to revise your life-plans to suit the circumstances and make changes wherever necessary, to take your plans towards your goal. You need to be flexible in your approach and bold enough to make changes where necessary. Changing plans is inevitable in life. Remember, how many times you had to change your plans about studies, jobs or marriage? Sometimes we abandon our plans when our initial actions do not encourage us. But most often we revise our plans or think of alternatives. In the same way, be prepared to revise your plans to realise your dreams, if required.

Don't look for perfection in all that you do. Accept the fact that things will not run perfectly. Recognise that neither your actions nor the finished product need to be perfect. If you aim perfection the fear of failure may haunt you. Instead, aim to complete the task. That itself is an accomplishment, because what was put off for a long time is now got done. After successfully completing a part of your dream project, reward yourself with anything you like—sweets, drinks, whatever. This will encourage you to take up the remaining work, if not bigger goals in life.

How this writer realised his dream

It takes a rare dream to inspire anyone to realise it. You must have heard of a lot of stories, how people have done it. But how will you know the actual process of realisation of such a wishful fantasy? Any description without first hand account will be bland and tasteless like a dish without salt. So, let me spice it up with a small dream of mine, that took considerable part of my life to shape into a reality:

> Sometime ago I stumbled upon a rare coin of Chandragupta Vikramaditya that came up for sale. This cute little piece, made of pure gold, is highly valuable. Since coin-collection is my hobby, I seized the opportunity and purchased it, though I couldn't afford it. Immediately I researched the available literature on Gupta coinage, wrote an article and got it published: Reminders of a golden regime (The Hindu, March 17,1991). Striking features of handsome king on the obverse, and auspicious image of goddess Lakshmi on the reverse, were so stunning that they invoked a sense of pleasure and enchantment that brooked my aesthetic brilliance. My fascination with it seemed like a silly obsession, but it soon grew into a surprising dream : How wonderful it would be if I could see these delightful pictures on the

jacket of a numismatic book? Yes, I was determined to realise it.

This is how my dream-project began. I started purchasing old coins representing various kingdoms. These ancient coins are very expensive. And if they are made of silver or gold, they cost a fortune; you will have to pay through your nose. Soon I realised that it is going to be a very difficult task, because they are not easily available. But if I want to realise my dream, I will have to get them somehow. To purchase the coins I was looking for, I had to visit all sorts of remote places: antique dealers, hobby specialists, *kabaadiwalahs* and even pavement vendors. It required a lot of effort, patience, persistence and tenacity. The time I could devote to this activity was very scanty, because I had to spend a lot of time for the more important pursuits of life. Yet, I could do it because my project was spread over a long period of time. The final ensemble of my beautiful coins was simply amazing! These charming pieces are not only enthralling to the coin-collectors but also delightful to the history-loving general public as well. Since writing a book like this, in one stretch, is really difficult, I decided to break it down into small manageable tasks. Researched about the coinage of ancient empires, wrote articles and got them published, one by one; thanks to, The Hindu, The Economic Times and Deccan Chronicle. Over a period of ten years I was able to publish seven articles.

Soon the time was ripe to put them together. Since the articles were not sufficient to form a book, I wrote seven more essays. I found a professional photographer, and got excellent close-up pictures of the required coins. But I did not have sufficient number of pictures of the gold coins of Guptas and the Vijayanagar empire. I obtained them with the courtesy of the Coin Keeper of A.P. State Museum. I edited the manuscript and tried various publishers until it was accepted. After a long wait of three years, my book was out in October 2003: *Coin Splendour: A Journey into the Past* (Abhinav Publications, New Delhi). It's a large format (28x22.5 cm) hard cover edition, printed on art paper. What a delightful piece for a debut! I was thrilled to see it showcased among the new arrivals at The Book Point. At last, I was greatly pleased to see the beautiful pictures of my favourite gold coin on the title page and the back page of its jacket. Like the metamorphosis of a caterpillar into a beautiful butterfly, my dream is now transformed into a wonderful reality.

Yes, my dream has come true at last—after twelve years! I have no words to describe what I felt that day! I was indeed overjoyed with a sense of achievement. I was virtually flying on the clouds wondering the myriad hues of the iridescent rainbow on the joyful horizon. Come, spread your wings. You too can fly, high in the sky!

When dreams become goals: The fuzzy logic

Our dreams are actually our flights of fancy always in the realms of half-mystery and half-fantasy. It is a fuzzy state that needs to be crystallised and clarified before we formulate our goals in life.

We pass through various stages of life from infancy to adulthood. At every stage we keep dreaming and forming life-goals. It is quite natural that our goals keep changing as we grow. In most cases, we formulate our life-goals at the stage of adolescence. In our formative years, the picture of our goals always looks fuzzy, and the realm of their possibility is never clear to us. That's the reason why we tinker with many things at a time, without settling on anything. In the meanwhile our needs keep changing as we grow. Then we see the necessity to blend life-goals with our needs.

Let me tell you a story. A sixteen-year-old girl, just come of age, met with an elderly lady who asked her, "Will you marry my son?" With a twinkle in her eye the girl asked, "How does he look? Is he handsome, good looking." By the time she was twenty, another lady asked her the same question: "Will you marry my son?" Having paused for a while, the girl snapped back, " What is he doing? How much does he get? Is he in a good position?" By the time she was thirty five, another lady asked her, "Will you marry my son?" Without losing time, the girl asked eagerly, "Where is he? Is he here?" Anybody could sense the urgency in her tone and voice. This is how the pressing needs prompt us to compromise on anything we could lay our hands on. The story did not end there. The girl remained unmarried for a long time. And by the time she was forty-five another lady asked, "Will you marry my son, a widower with two kids?" The spinster listened attentively and reflected for a while: "How rich is he? Does he have lots of properties?," she inquired politely. This is how our changing needs, at all stages of life, make us look for different things among the available options. No wonder, our goals keep changing all the time depending on our needs.

When my son was playing, someone asked him: " What will you become when you grow up?" He replied immediately, " I'll become a driver. I love to drive this big double-decker bus." When he grew up, he majored in psychology like his father, but finally he ended up as a computer professional. That's how many people land up their careers capturing available opportunities. No wonder our dreams and goals keep changing with the times.

Young people do not discriminate a dream from a goal; for some of them their dream is their goal—a dream-goal. A young man may have a dream: to become a doctor of eminence, to care for the health of people, to make a difference to the world around. This is indeed a dream having the potential to become a life-goal. Look at scientists, doctors, sports-persons, artists, poets, writers; their goals are mostly related to their professions that engage them for a life time. And they do have other pursuits that become secondary goals.

But our dreams need not lead to such life-goals. Our goals can be varied—success-goals, happiness-goals, profit-goals, money-goals. Their importance keep changing as we grow. Keep a track of the changes in your life and the changing dreams and goals.

When dreams merge with goals they become our life

Some people are able to knit their dreams around their lives; for them their life is their dream, and their life-goal is like chasing the biggest dream. Naturalist Henry David Thoreau says, "If one advances confidently in the direction of his dreams and endeavours to live the life which he has imagined, he will meet with success unexpected in common hour". You must have heard of many Indians who realised their dreams in their life time. Jamsetji Nasarwanji Tata, a man of great vision, pioneered the steel industry in India. His dreams, combined with his enterprising spirit, gave birth to many companies such as Tata Steel, Tata Motors, Tata Tea, Tata Telcom, and Tata Consultancy Services, etc. Dhirubhai Ambani, an ambitious man with business dreams, had built single handed the Reliance Group of Industries from scratch to a Rs 90,000 crore enterprise. N.R. Narayana Murty, an ambitious technocrat realised his entrepreneurial dreams by setting up the software giant Infosys Technologies. The story of the richest Indian Azim H. Premji of Wipro Corporation is equally impressive. You must be wondering what had driven these people to achieve such great things in their lifetime. The secret behind their achievements perhaps lies in the broader vision of their dreams and their solid commitment to realise them. If they could do such wonderful things in one lifetime, why not you and me? You must be wondering, what is it that we have to do ? "We need to think big and bold in what we do," advises Ratan Tata, chairman of Tata Motors. Perhaps, that is what we have to do when it comes to deciding life goals.

"Shoot at a lion and let it miss; but don't try to hunt a jackal," is a proverb. Our headmaster used to explain its purport: you may miss the shot, but it will surely increase your self-esteem because you have attempted something great. Even if you miss the shot, you stand high in the eyes of the world. He used to persuade us to attempt I.A.S. with his simple logic: "Work hard, in all probability, you will be through; even if you miss the rank, who knows, you might get into the allied services." Then he used to crack a joke: " If you dream high and aim to become a collector, you will at least get a bill-collector's job. But if you wish to become a bill-collector, God knows where you will end up." Yes, we need to think big before we achieve.

Life goals make us happy

Behind tears there is past and beyond dreams there is future that begins now. That's what makes us formulate future goals. Behind goals there is an unconditional hope that looks forward to success and fulfilment in life. All this is because, " The human spirit needs to accomplish, to achieve, to triumph, to be happy," says Ben Stein, the Speech Writer to Richard Nixon.

"In every human being is a predisposition toward achievement of goals," says Maxwell Maltz, the Psycho-cybernetics guru. It is true because, there is no achievement in life without goals. Ultimately it is the achievement of goals that makes us happy. "If you want to have a happy life, tie it to a goal, not to people or things," advises Albert Einstein, one of the greatest scientists and philosophers of our time.

"Happiness does not come from doing an easy task but from the afterglow of satisfaction that comes after the achievement of a difficult task that demanded our best," says American author Theodore I Rubin. "It is one of the strange ironies of this strange life that those who work the hardest, who subject themselves to the strict discipline, who give up pleasurable things in order to achieve a goal are the happiest men," says Brutus Hamilton, decathlete and coach for US Olympic Decathlon Team.

"Men must have goals, which in their eyes merit effort and commitment and they must believe and their efforts will win them self-respect and respect of others," says Professor John Gardner of Stanford University.

Short-term and long-term goals

"You must have goals for everyday living", says Psycho-cybernetics guru Maxwell Maltz. "It is not enough to select goals; your next step is to focus your attention on them with a steady gaze, and reach them. This is the only way to get real enjoyment from your life activities...Plan your day, set your goals; tomorrow you will set more goals. Each day you will find something to enjoy."

It is more important to take small steps now than to think too far into the future. That is, we have to think of achieving small goals relating to immediate needs first while we keep in mind long-term life-goals. Setting small goals does not mean we are less ambitious. It only means that we are trying first to achieve what is within our reach. It does not bar us from trying higher goals. These small beginnings will translate into short-term goals. They keep changing depending on urgency, unlike the important long-term goals. Therefore, we have to ensure that our short-term goals blend smoothly with long-term goals.

Never forget the *importance* of long-term goals. According to Management guru, Stephen R. Covey, efficient self-managers spend more time on important life-goals. When you take up a long-range plan on goals, you have time on your side. So, don't get distracted by trivial things, however urgent they may look. Devote less time on things that are neither urgent nor important. Think of the priorities in life and work out your life-plans accordingly. Always keep in mind how you can prevent or solve problems and produce results. Build a good network of friends and relatives, you never know when you need them. In the process, relax when overworked; seek recreation whenever you can and never forget to enjoy life.

Long-term goals may take years to accomplish unlike short-term goals that can be achieved within a few weeks or months. It is indeed a good strategy to break down long-term goals into short-term goals; which in turn can be divided further into manageable tasks—both large and small. Achievement of long-term goals often requires some team effort. Involve your spouse, family members, relatives and friends in all your plans and efforts. Combined team effort, rather than your individual brilliance, can result in wonderful results. Long-term goals are usually difficult to pursue, take a long time to achieve. They should be pursued with great patience and perseverance . "Patience is power; with time and patience mulberry leaf becomes silk," says a Chinese proverb. Yes, if you have patience and persistence everything becomes possible.

Give top priority to your life-goal
Human beings are full of hope, intelligence, boundless potential. We are inspired by our dreams to achieve, not only for personal glory but to secure common good. " Dreams pass into reality of action. From the action stems the dream again and this interdependence produces the highest form of living," says American novelist Anias Nin.

Look at the examples of great people. Preacher Martin Luther King Jr says, "I had a dream." His dream was about liberating his people—the black Americans, who were slogging even though slavery was abolished long ago. He dedicated his life to see that his dream comes true. We know how Mohandas Karamchand Gandhi dedicated his life to the cause of liberating his country.

Consider the example of Wright brothers, who dreamt of achieving personal goals of building flying machines that serve the humanity at large.

"You don't have to invent the airplane or create an empire to pursue a big dream of your own," say James Chimpy and Nitin Nohria in *The Arc of Ambition*. Your dream may not be that lofty, all the same it is important for you. Your dream may be very personal one, relating to you or your family—an exciting career, a dream house, excellent education for children and their decent settlement, a peaceful retirement. You may even be dreaming of other short-term projects.

If your dream is important for you, incorporate it in your life-plans. The first thing in life is to consider priorities, whatever be your career aspirations or goals in life. Otherwise, if you allow trivial things to consume your life time, your dream will never come true. When you give top priority to the task of realising your dream, all other things in life become secondary. And you will see that everything serves the purpose of your dream-project. Work steadily till you realise your dream or achieve your goal, one after the other. Remember, no dream is small, if it can give you joy and happiness. But always dream and try to realise what you dream, no matter how small.

Take your life-goal as a challenge
According to well-known author Richard Bach anyone can achieve anything in the world. "The trick is one should stop seeing oneself" as trapped inside a limited body. "We must try to overcome our limitations." If we can see unlimited potential in us , we will be able to realise our dreams and achieve our goals. Since you do not know what potential is hidden inside, it is not wise to underestimate yourself.

"It may shock many to know that beliefs about life are not necessarily the truth," says Psychic Counsellor Pamala Oslie in

Make Your Dreams Come True. She poses three questions: "Do you believe that you have little or no control over your destiny? Do you often feel you are a victim of circumstances, society or other people? Do you see you are responsible for creating your life experiences?" If we are limitless in our capabilities why do we limit ourselves? Answer: "We don't trust ourselves." Add to it "critical self judgement and suppression of inner voice" to complicate the matters. She says, "You can change the beliefs that limit you."

Your dream is actually the reality in waiting! "There are some people who live in a dream world; there are some people who face reality; and there are some who turn one into the other," says American author Douglas Everett. Don't be afraid of the space between dreams and reality. If you can dream it you can make it true in real life. Remember, future belongs to those who believe in the potential of their dreams.

Set realistic and achievable goals: plan your life around them
Aiming high is laudable, but very lofty goals are generally unrealistic; where targets are easier to set but difficult to achieve. When we are unable to accomplish them, we are easily disappointed; and we may even question our capabilities. In the process we may experience a lot of stress. "Choose your goals and make sure that they are really your own, not imposed by others" advises Canadian Endocrinologist Dr. Hans Selye, an authority on stress. This is important because it will help you achieve anything without much stress.

Set realistic goals and assume a reasonable amount of responsibility for the consequences of your actions. The hallmark of a realistic goal is its possibility. If a man has a realistic goal with the possibility of success, he will be determined to achieve it. What follows is a flurry of concerted actions with persistent effort. That's what increases the chances of achieving success. Have a clear idea of your goal or dream project and the required abilities, skills and effort to achieve it. Set achievable goals, however small they may be, and fix targets at a reasonably comfortable level. This is what we call realistic approach to setting goals. "Happiness, wealth and success are the by-products of goal setting," says Career counselor John Condry.

Means for achieving goals is crucial

"I have been always learning great lessons from that one principle," says Swami Vivekananda, " and it appears to me that all the secret of success is there: *to pay attention to the means as to the end* (italics are mine). Whenever failure comes, if we analyse critically, in ninety-nine per cent of the cases we shall find that it was because we did not pay attention to the means. If we take care of the cause, the effect will take care of itself. The realisation of the ideal is the effect. The means are the cause: attention to means, therefore, is the secret of life." Yes, it is crucial to pay attention to the means—money, materials, methods and other resources. Therefore, examine the means required to realise your dreams. They are very important because your success depends on them.

Take advantage of opportunities

"Seek, ye shall find," says Jesus of Nazareth. True, how can you ever find anything if you don't look for it, let alone an opportunity? If you are wrapped up in your own shell you will never see an opportunity. Finding it is a matter of perception. It is easier to grasp an opportunity if you know how it looks like. Get your neck out and look around in the big wide world. "Luck means being in the right place at the right time to see an opportunity," says British Field Marshal Viscount Slim.

"Effective people are not problem minded; they are opportunity minded," says Peter Drucker, a well-known management expert. Psychologist Edward de Bono of Oxford University recognised the importance of looking for profitable opportunities. But he warns that you can reap benefits only if your *perception* of opportunity matches with the *reality* of its existence. In his book *Opportunities,* he gives many examples of business ventures that were virtual disasters for the single reason that they were based on unrealistic obsessions of opportunities. It is good to take advantage of opportunities. But it is not wise to wait for opportunities, doing nothing. A Polish proverb says, "if there is no wind, row." If no opportunity is visible, keep working. You never know when it will show up. "The golden opportunity you are seeking is yourself," says American author Orison Swett Marden." It is not in your environment, it is not in luck or chance, or the help of others, it is in yourself alone."

Take calculated risk: rewards can be high
"There are risks and costs to a programme of action. But they are far less than the long range risks and costs of comfortable inaction," says the late US president John F. Kennedy. According to Psychologist David C. McClelland of Harvard University, calculated risk is one of the important qualities of high achievers. It goes hand in hand with reasonable rewards.

No one can afford to be reluctant to take risk when so much in life is at stake. "Without risk you have only stable conditions and you know the stables are not for humans," says American writer Judith M Bardwick in *Seeking Calm in the Storm.* "So push beyond the envelope of your comfort zone." Great rewards can accrue by taking high risk; but everyone has to decide at what level of risk one is comfortable, yet the rewards are substantial. This is what we call calculated risk.

Find joy in the process of achieving your goals: enjoy the endeavour
The glory of winning or the agony of losing are but short-lived reactions after considerable effort. "The moment of victory is much too short to live for that and nothing else," as observed by

tennis legend Martina Navratilova. Looking forward to success is no doubt exciting; but the real joy is in the effort and endeavour we put in, to achieve our goals. Reaching the goal or achieving success are only events that we rejoice for a few moments; whereas it is the exhilarating journey towards the goal that gives unlimited joy because it is spread over considerably long time—may be a life time!

Happiness comes along with us all the way through our journey in this life. Joy is actually hidden in our struggle to succeed in life. We derive greatest happiness in the course of overcoming the hurdles to success. "Happiness is a journey, not a destination:" There is a lot of truth in this saying, because we feel happy when we are in the process of achieving goals. We experience real happiness on the way to success; and when we reach our goal we are no doubt overjoyed to celebrate success. Again the joy returns when we recollect the happiest moments we spent during the course of our struggle to achieve success. In short, we enjoy the endeavour more than the joy we get when we reach the goals!

Joyful moments are disguised in our determination, dedication and hard work. The joy that comes along with whole-hearted endeavour is incredibly adorable! And memories of such a joyful struggle are worth rejoicing time and time again!

Success and Failure Are Relative

> Believe that you succeed, you will succeed.
> *Dale Carnegie (1888-1955)*
> Pioneer of Personality development

> There is only one success—to be able to spend the life in your own way.
> *Christopher Morley (1890-1957)*
> American Writer

Short life but great expectations

We don't realise the change in our lives that comes with time. Along with physical changes comes growth and maturity in our personality. Our values get modified and our goals and expectations keep changing. Our changing expectations lead our actions and life in the long run. "One isn't born oneself," reminds Nobel laureate V.S. Naipaul. "One is born with a mass of expectations, a mass of other people's ideas – give and you have to work it all." Many things you expect to see in life will never be visible unless you look for them.

If you have too many expectations in life, it is difficult to meet all of them. Many expectations deserve to be surpassed. It is more important to target a few things at a time, than too many.

"What we anticipate seldom occurs, but what we least expect generally happens," reminds former British Prime Minister Benjamin Disraeli. How true! We attempt many things but only to find the results inversely proportional to our expectations. Another tragedy is that we are never prepared to face what we expect. Since many unexpected things are likely to happen, you must be prepared to deal with them.

Realistic expectations and achievements

"You will never be happier than you expect. To change your happiness, change your expectation," says American actress Bette Davis. Remember, no one is in control of your expectations but you; therefore, you have the power to change anything about yourself or your expectations in life. Change your expectations and see that they are realistic. "Your own expectations are the key to the whole business of mental health. If you expect to be happy, healthy and fulfilled in life, then most likely it will work out that way," says Psychotherapist Wayne Dyer.

Unrealistic high expectations and inappropriate actions cause failures

All of us have certain beliefs about the world. Many times the reality out there differs with what we believe it to be. Every time we close the door on *reality* it comes through the window; but we foolishly ignore its presence. When the gap between our *beliefs* and *reality* widens we tend to have unrealistic expectations in our life. Most often, we fail because we are unable to handle the difficulties in realistic ways.

"A great obstacle to happiness is to anticipate too great a happiness," says French author (Bernard de Bovier de la) Fontenelle. That is unrealistic. Again, if our unrealistic expectations overweigh our talents, it is difficult to meet all of them. In this context, British author Samuel Johnson says, "expectations improperly indulged must end up in disappointment". Psychologist Edward de Bono says, "Unhappiness is best defined as the difference between our talents and our expectations."

Success and happiness in life

"What man really wants is a creative challenge with sufficient skills to bring him within the reach of success so that he may have expanding joy of achievement," says Fay B Nash. Yes, there is always an inalienable link between success and happiness. Sweet smile of success indicates inner happiness. What constitutes success varies from person to person. "Success is getting what you want. Happiness is wanting and being content with what you get," says Professor Bernard Meltzer. According to Maharshi Mahesh Yogi, "Success in anything is through happiness."

The common idea that success spoils people making them vain, egoistic and self-complacent is erroneous; on the contrary it makes them, for most part, humble, tolerant, and kind. Failure makes people bitter and cruel.

Abstract nature of success and happiness

"My goal in life is to achieve success and happiness," is a common statement we often hear from people. It implies that they are chasing success and happiness as if they are separate entities having independent existence in the world. We all commit the same mistake while using the words 'success' or 'happiness' as if these are the things we are after. This is because we have a problem in understanding the real meaning of these words.

'Success' and 'happiness' are abstract nouns. " An abstract noun is usually the name of a quality, action, or state considered apart from the object to which it belongs." It is indeed the most authoritative definition by the well-known British grammarians P.C. Wren and H. Martin. 'Happiness' is derived from the adjective 'happy,' and 'success' is formed from the verb 'succeed.'

Happiness is a quality of being happy and it is a state of mind. Success is the result of action, it is also a state of mind.

When we say "I am happy" or "I feel happy," these words indicate how happy we are. Strictly speaking, it is not correct to say, "I have happiness;" because we are treating happiness as a separate thing which is not true. It is right to say, "I have succeeded in the examination" rather than saying, "I have achieved success." Here again we are committing the same mistake of treating success as if it is an independent entity. Yet, unmindful of this paradox, we all use these words. That's what creates problems in understanding 'success' and 'happiness'.

Success and failure are subjective reactions

What constitutes success varies from person to person. For some, success may mean gaining power or making lots of money. For someone it may be a personal honour like an Olympic gold medal or a Nobel Prize. For another person it may be a loving relationship with spouse or dear ones. Still there are others who look for peace and tranquillity in life. Personal definition of success changes from time to time as we grow in age. Eventually success is what we feel inside ourselves; it is all in our mind, not anywhere else—we must look deeply within ourselves, what we want in life and reflect on what really we mean by success.

"I really think happiness is closely aligned with success and may almost be an interchangeable synonym. Happiness, like success, also comes from doing what we feel called to do in life ; however, it is also obvious no one can experience one without the other," says American author Donna Fargo.

Hope of success and fear of failure

Do you worry about others' opinion about you? Do you have a reputation for excellence , but still feel incompetent? This is what Psychotherapist Professor Petruska Clarkson calls Achille's Syndrome in *How to Overcome Your Fear of Failure*. People with this syndrome "are seen by others as much more competent than they feel in themselves, and they exert inappropriate amounts of energy and tension to perform. Or are exhausted and drained by success instead of building up their confidence." Why so? This is because, "they develop defences to cover up what they feel is their Achilles heel." She says this is their "psuedo-competency." For " the mark of genuinely competent professionals is to know what they can do and cannot do, as well as being able to judge the competency of their peers and colleagues in the same professional group."

Success in solving problems in life

Life is a series of problems. If life were to be simple without problems, it won't be called life, after all. What is life without hurdles? Without real action, it will be nothing more than a passive sequence of events. Life can be so boring without adventure; we get tired of it very easily. When we get anything with least effort we feel it wasn't worth it, however precious it is. But we prize even a trivial thing when it is won by hard work. We will not appreciate the value of anything obtained without effort on our part. "Happiness includes chiefly the idea of satisfaction after full honest effort," says American novelist (Enoch) Arnold Bennet. "No one can possibly be satisfied and no one can be happy who feels that in some paramount affairs he failed to take up the challenge of life." Yes, with challenge comes achievement, and with strife comes satisfaction and joy. That is the reason why we love to encounter challenges in life. Overcoming hurdles gives a sense of success and achievement.

In our quest to explore the world, we are curious to find exciting frontiers. We try to do many things with the premise that 'everything is possible and no problem is insurmountable.' That's why we equip ourselves to meet any challenge in life. Dealing with obstacles and manoeuvering our way through the world are noble tasks that call forth our hidden potential. To face every problem in life, we must make it possible to manifest the best of what we are: our talents and abilities, our hopes and dreams, our aspirations and ambitions, our dedication and hard work. Perhaps that is the reason why we always look for problems, as if it is our mission in life.

"For a long time it had seemed to me that life was about to begin—real life," says Father Alfred D'souza. "But there was always some obstacle on the way, something to gotten first, some unfinished business, time still to be served, a debt to be paid. Then life would begin. At last it dawned on me that these obstacles were my life." Yes, life is a series of problems; and finding solutions is our job in life. In the process this gives a sense of success and achievement.

Problems that come up in life go far beyond imagination. Yet the human genius finds creative solutions for the sheer pleasure of achievement. Every time we face a tough problem we try to find a way to solve it. If a solution already exists, we will try to find a better solution. Where it is not available, we will invent one. When we see that no solution is possible to a problem or there is nothing we can do about it, we will find a way of managing the situation. It looks as if we require problems to keep ourselves busy in life. It appears our happiness requires problems.

"Happiness is like those palaces in fairy tales guarded by dragons: we must fight in order to conquer it," says French author Alexandre Dumas. So let us not whimper or murmur when things seem tough. Let us put our 'shoulder to the wheel' and overcome the boulders on our path. Let us experience the excitement of every new challenge we face, and enjoy the thrill of success and joy in every solution we find. Overcoming problems brings growth, which is at the core of happiness.

Life is full of problems like thorns on a rose, yet we admire its beauty and enjoy its fragrance. Savouring life is like licking honey off the thorn, but the trick is to somehow overcome the thorny problems in life. "Life affords no higher pleasure than surmounting difficulties, passing from one step of success to another, forming new wishes and seeing them gratified," says British author Samuel Johnson. Overcoming the world is the essence of success in life.

Success in competition with others

Any effort made to compete with others brings complex dynamics to win over others. Wise king Solomon says, " Wisdom prevails over strength, knowledge over brute force. For wars are won by skillful strategy, victory is the fruit of long planning." This is mainly the domain of warlords and sports persons who are required to face adversaries or competitors. Yet, we all need to think of winning strategies whenever we face competition in life. But "The trouble with being in the rat race is that even if you win, you're still a rat," says American Comedian Lily Tomlin.

Those who compare themselves with others, struggle a lot to compete with others and somehow manage to achieve a bit of success in life. One-upmanship is a common game among those who pride in their superior talents. Its main aim is to put down others at any cost. Trying to outsmart others is sheer wastage of talents and resources. Since there is no end to comparison, people often end up in frustration because they cannot win them all. On the other hand, some people feel jealous of other's success, because they cannot compete with everybody. They often use unholy strategies to pull others down. Diane Kennedy author of *Loopholes of the Rich,* made a passing remark about Australians, who are said to believe in "cutting down the tall poppy." She says, "It is practically their moral responsibility to cut a friend down to size if the person starts rising over the present circumstances. Like crabs, they pull others back into the box, because they are afraid and also they don't want other guys to succeed, it means they would have to change themselves also," but that would be " a challenge to their own complacency."

Remember, you don't have to win everyone, every time, everywhere. You don't have to compete in order to enjoy life. Relax . If you really want to compete in this world, go ahead, compete with yourself, try to excel. Remember, you have the power to excel and the true greatness is in being superior to your previous self. And the real competition is between your past performance and the present effort to do better. This is more of a realistic strategy because it accepts the existence of greater talents in you. Exploring the undiscovered potential in yourself will actually fulfil the higher need for self-actualisation. This is more desirable than the struggle to compete with everybody around.

Belief in success is a pre-requisite
"They won because they think they can," says Roman poet Virgil while speaking of a winning team of a boat race. " We lost because we told ourselves we lost," says Russian author Leo Tolstoy in *War and Peace.* Yes, belief precedes our success and failure. Personality Development guru Dale Carnegie is right when he says, "Believe that you succeed, you will succeed." Belief in your ability to succeed is important. You must have an image of your success powerful enough to sustain effort through numerous setbacks.

"Faith in oneself ….is the best and safest course," says Michelangelo (di Lodovico Buonarroti Simoni), one of the greatest painters in the world. Yes, you must have belief in yourself and faith in your own abilities to achieve success. "Your abilities count , but the belief that you succeed affects whether or not you will succeed," says Psychologist Michael Sheier.

Know the ingredients of success
Most people are searching for the secret formula for success. What successful people have in common? The Gallup Organisation in

the US posed this question to 1500 professionally successful people. They found five factors that contribute to success: "commonsense, knowing your field, self-reliance, intelligence, and ability to get things done." They also found other factors that influence success: "leadership, creativity, relationships with others and, of course, luck." They say, " If you cultivate these traits chances are you will succeed. You might even find yourself listed in *Who is Who* some day."

Studies at the University of California yielded similar results. Psychologist Charles Garfield studied outstanding achievers in nearly all walks of life. He found traits *that can be learned by anyone*:

- Lead well-rounded life
- Select a career you care about
- Rehearse each challenging task mentally
- Seek results, not perfection
- Be willing to risk
- Don't underestimate your potential
- Compete with yourself not with others

American writer Morton Hunt says, " Such are the skills of the high performers. If you want to make more of your talents— to live up to your potential—then learn to use them."

Success is a bumpy road: discover the joy on the way

No one can achieve success without setbacks and failures. The bumpy road to success is not strewn with roses; instead it has sudden and hidden pitfalls. They scare the people who are afraid of them. You have to pass through this rough terrain with 'indomitable will and indefatigable zeal' till you reach your goal. Lift up yourself with the spirit of enthusiasm, rise above the obstacles and zoom ahead with your determination. We derive greatest happiness in the course of overcoming the hurdles in our life. Happiness comes along with us in our journey through life.

Joy is actually hidden in our struggle to succeed in life. We experience real happiness on the way to success. Again the joy returns when we recollect the happiest moments we spent during the course of our struggle to achieve success.

Failures before success are very common
"Life does not accommodate you, it shatters you. It is meant to, and it couldn't do it better. Every seed destroys its container or else there is no fruition," says American psychologist Florida Scott-Maxwell. Yes, painful experience of difficulties and setbacks are inevitable before we succeed in life. These experiences should not be treated as setbacks or failures; rather they should be considered as part of our learning by trial and error.

The word 'failure' is misunderstood most of the time. When we slip on the steps, do we consider it a failure on our part? It is more proper to call it an accident, not a failure. Certainly it is not a reason to doubt our ability to walk. Many times we encounter setbacks when we attempt difficult tasks; but we should not consider them as failures.

Just as a child stumbles while learning to walk, we all trip sometimes while attempting to succeed in life. When we encounter obstacles, we often stumble and fall; but we should not consider them as failures. We should see them as delightful baby steps, on the path towards success. These stumbling blocks should be considered as a stepping stones to success. Success does not come without experiencing setbacks, adversities and obstacles. This is authenticated by Steve Young in his book, *Great Failures of the Extremely Successful: Mistakes, Adversity, Failure and Other Stepping Stones to Success*. According to him "a failure is mankind's greatest ignored resource". As American political writer Georges Clemenceau puts it, "A man's life is interesting primarily when he failed–for it is a sign that he tried to surpass himself." Pop singer Celine Dion puts it, "The real failure is not knowing how to be happy."

Don't cry over spilt milk

American author Ann Landers once narrated a real life incident in which her English teacher taught the futility of rehashing the past: "One day, as the students filed into her classroom, we noticed on her desk a bottle of milk standing in a heavy jar. "This morning," she announced, " I'm going to teach you a lesson that has nothing to do with English, but it has a lot to do with life. She picked up the bottle of milk and crashed against the inside of the stone jar. "The lesson is" she said, "don't cry over spilt milk." Then she invited us to look at the wreckage."

"I want all of you to remember this ," she said. "Would any of you attempt to restore the bottle to its original form? Does it do any good to wish the bottle had not been broken? Look at this mess! You can moan about it forever, but it won't put the bottle back together again. Remember this broken bottle of milk when something happens in your life that nothing can undo." Every time you think of a frustrating experience, remind yourself the story of the broken bottle of milk in the stone jar. Just as you can't restore the broken bottle, you can't do anything about your frustrations. This kind of thinking can help you remain steady and calm.

A familiar quotation comes to mind – "I cried because I had no shoes, until I met a man who had no feet." Yes, when we know the other side of the story, our frustrating experience takes on a different meaning. We can't appreciate light if we haven't known darkness. Nor can we appreciate warmth if we have never suffered cold. American poet Anne Bradstreet says, " If we had no winter, the spring would not be pleasant; if we did not sometimes have taste of adversity, prosperity would not be so welcome." We need some failures and frustrating experiences that allow us to appreciate and admire our triumphant achievements. If our failures and disappointments have served that purpose we must be thankful!

Don't give up: try again

Suppose you could not unscrew a stubborn nut. It is quite natural that you get a jittery feeling that does not subside until you unscrew it. You need not lose heart simply because your first attempt did not yield the desired result. It does not mean, you don't have the ability nor it is a failure on your part. You don't have to feel defeated by the insignificant nut! "Being defeated is only a temporary condition. Giving it up makes it permanent," says American writer Marylin vos Savant. Don't ever give up. Try again. Perhaps the solution lies in the use of an appropriate tool or proper method. The moment you recognise the solution, success will unfold on its own.

"You can't advance in life without that jittery feeling. You'll never eliminate anxiety by avoiding the things that caused it. You can't learn if you don't try," says American musician and author James Lincoln Collier. "Don't be crushed if you fail," says American journalist Dan Rather. " If you indulge yourself that way, you'll never put yourself in a pressure situation again, you'll never grow. If you do fail, go back over, find what happened. Think of everything , including the moment things started to go bad and why. Work out. Try again." Don't let fear of failure stop you from trying at all. Remember, every failed attempt is worth a sincere try. If you are already trying, try harder till you achieve success.

A failure may darken sentiment: but it can teach how to survive

A failure may immobilise us for a while, but it is not strong enough to force us to retreat. Our first reaction to a failure may be frustration and disappointment; but it should not push us to doubt our ability to succeed. It may trigger clouds of negative feelings that darken our sentiment. It may disturb our mind and distort our thoughts just as the smoked glass windows. We have to scrub them off as soon as possible; otherwise light won't come in. It is difficult to have a clear perspective. We will not be able to grasp what our failures can teach. Failures often offer lessons to overcome them; and they show the way to our survival.

We are taught lessons in school before we are required to take a test. But the reverse is true in life: we have to take the test first, and learn the lessons later. Failure in any unprepared attempt is the result of a real test in life. That makes you learn what has gone wrong. American author Vic Sussman says, "Don't Fear Failure" (*Reader's Digest,* Jan.'91). She says, "It is the normal way to map the unknown—and can be your greatest teacher." You should therefore try to reduce your fear of failure and learn from your experience to make a smooth journey. *Successful people are not the people who don't fail; they are the people who learned from their failures.*

"You must learn from the mistakes of others," says American humorist and author Samuel Levenson. "You can't possibly live long enough to make them all by yourself." Your learning must include your mistakes as well as those of others. Yes, a failure can become success if you learn from it.

Failure as a means to achieve success
Billi PS Lim, a Malaysian self-management guru, has a unique philosophy that has different focus from the so-called success gurus: It focuses on failure as a means to success. He says, "Seminars on success never prepare anyone for failure." He believes that "failure is necessary to achieve success and maintain it. Otherwise there is a danger of becoming arrogant or becoming afraid of losing again." He says, "Success is not the goal; but journey towards the goal."

It is difficult to achieve failure
Have you ever wondered how to be a failure? "It requires as much skill to become a truly outstanding failure as it does to become

truly great in any field," says American writer Charles Brower in *"How to be a Failure"* (*Reader's Digest*, Feb.'66). "It needs a disciplined approach to achieve this goal."

"First you must get rid of the universal belief that success is desirable," says Brower. Then you should avoid doing a real day's work for a day's pay. A half-done job is good enough. Flee from responsibility. Don't be a yes man. Don't say "yes, sir". Learn to say "yes, but…" If you are an executive you can paralyse progress and avoid decisions by saying, "Yes, but I don't think we should rush to this." Don't fall in love with your work, for real enemy of failure is the thrill of achievement. More promising failures have gone wrong because they discovered that achievement is fun than for any single reason. So watch out for the moment when pride begins to creep into your work. Avoid the feeling of wanting to tell some one that you have had really a good day.

"Finally, there are a few things, you ought to forget right at the start. Forget what some poet has said: " Not failure, low aim is crime." And forget what another poet has said: "God give me hills to climb, strength for climbing." Forget what Alexander Graham Bell says: " Don't keep forever on the public road, going only where others have gone. Leave the beaten path occasionally and dive into the woods. You will be certain to find something you have never seen before. One discovery will lead to another, and before you know it, you will have something worth thinking about it. All really big discoveries are the result of thought." The level to strive is "average." So you will have plenty of company in your happy and obscure mediocrity.

"There are several other advantages of becoming a failure. Successful people work like mad, often for others. Failures do not have to work at all. Successes often so wound up in their jobs they cannot sleep well. Failures can usually sleep, even in the day time. If you are a success your problems will become bigger and bigger. You may have to cope with the whole national budget or run a company that has problems in 20 different nations. And nobody cares. And there is no government department devoted to the problems of successes. Whereas, if you are a failure, everybody worries about you. The whole government studies your case."

"I'd rather be a failure at something I enjoy, than be a success at something I hate," says American comic actor George Burns. Then, why not prefer failure if it can give pleasure and joy!

Joy is in bouncing back to life

You are not a born-expert at doing anything perfect. Expertise is something you develop by trial and error. Very rarely one achieves success in the first attempt, more so when one tries new things. The bumpy road to success is never without pitfalls. Setbacks are inevitable in all human endeavours. Even successful people encounter failures very often. "Everyone gets a chance, no one lives a fail-proof life forever," says Professor Amitai Etzioni. Yes, we all make bad choices, even stupid mistakes. But we don't have to be scared of the imaginary consequences.

There is no point in getting worried about setbacks and failed attempts, or impatient about accomplishment. Think with a cool head and refocus on your dream goals. Note down your weak points, and try to strengthen those areas. Make required changes in your approach that could help you avoid failures. As you work through the setbacks that come up, you will know your limits as well as strengths. "Once we accept our limits we go beyond them," says Irish Playwright Brenden Francis. As you learn from mistakes and failures, you will find how to make your dreams come true. See them as your opportunities to learn how to succeed. Learn what you can from your setbacks and mistakes. Learn from them why you failed and what is required to succeed. Revise your plans and priorities, and perfect your approach. Once you realise your dreams, you will discover the person you are designed to be.

A few unsuccessful attempts and consequent failures and criticism may induce fear of failure and related negative feelings. You may even feel dumped. Yes, you have the feeling of clinging to the cliff as your life tumbles and rolls down, slipping away from your hand. What is important is never to dilute your hope of success. You may have lost the battle, but there is still some hope to win the war. Don't ever give in or give up.

Get rid of the blues of the past failures. No point in indulging in regrets. So, don't get perturbed when faced with difficulties. Stop whining, hold your fortitude, especially when things are not going right for you. This is the time to remember that within all of us lie untapped wellsprings of strength that can sustain us in times of trouble.

In such frustrating situations summon your courage and self-confidence, bring out your inner strength. Reinforce them with indomitable spirit and indefatigable zeal. Be strong and give life a fight. Get fired up, get started again, fold up your sleeves, pull up your socks, get down to work. Be in the driver's seat and ignite the engine of survival instinct and gear up your inner strength. If necessary, take your own time to equip and prepare yourself, but strike at the right moment, with full force. Transcend adversity and rise to the top. As the famous football Coach Vince Lombardi puts it, "The real glory is being knocked down to your knees and then coming back."

Though you are taking a lot of risk there is no guarantee that your efforts will pay off in the very first attempt. Don't get discouraged, because this happens with all serious attempts. You must have heard of the story of King Robert Bruce of Scotland who was once imprisoned by his enemies. He observed a spider in the prison cell, trying to climb a wall with the help of yarn spun from its own saliva. Every time it tried, it failed miserably. But the failures did not induce any feelings of defeat; nor had any effect on its morale. Rather they only reinforced its determination to try again and increased its persistence. It tried again and again, with renewed effort, until it succeeded in the seventeenth attempt. Having drawn his inspiration from the spider, Bruce was able to escape from the prison after several unsuccessful attempts though.

It is important to realise that all human beings are endowed with the instinct to survive. Even in the 2004 Tsunami disaster, people struck by mishap did not give up. They pulled together amazingly, adapted, worked hard and bounced back. Remember, you too can do it, no matter how severe is the calamity. Not all disasters have the quality of 'sudden impact' on life. Most of them give sufficient time to tackle them, so that you can think with a cool head how best to meet the challenge.

Bouncing back from failure is indeed a daunting task. This is what we call resilience: the ability to thrive in adverse conditions, cope with crises and bounce back stronger than before. It will help us cope with adversities when we face them. We can survive failures and adversities and make them work for us. Actually, failures bring out our inner potential— hidden resources, qualities, abilities, and strengths—that we did not know we possessed. The trick is to look for insights from failed attempts and pursue the task with resilience and renewed effort.

Dealing with failures is a very tough job that calls for tremendous effort. Once again let us consider the rock solid determination of bicycle repairmen Orville Wright and his brother Wilber Wright. In spite of set backs, they were able to ride a flying machine made by their own efforts. If you are interested, find some time to read about their failed attempts and their frustrations. After every attempt, they examined what caused the failure and learned how to overcome it. They tried every possible thing with renewed effort to make it a success. It is indeed a story of repeated failures that yielded final success.

Have you heard of the story of a living legend John Forbes Nash Jr., a mathematical genius? Having suffered a serious mental breakdown for several years, he bounced back to win Nobel Prize for Economics in 1994. If you can spare some time, read about it in Sylvia Nasar's *A Beautiful Mind,* that inspired a Hollywood film by the same title starring Russell Crowe. Every human being is capable of bouncing back to joyful life; it is a testimony to human resilience. Don't ever have any doubts about your come back powers.

Divert energies generated by frustration to achievable goals
Failures and setbacks often generate feelings of frustration. The immediate thing to do is to cool down and think what you can do about the thing that is frustrating. Focus on the problem, and examine the causes of failure. May be it calls for a little more patience, some more effort and practice. Examine what other choices are available to you. Think about new strategies. Try to harness your frustration to your best advantage.

It is important to remember that every frustrating experience can push you to the brink of collapse. But the most surprising element is in its ability to generate great amounts of energy to fight back. Unsuccessful people often waste these energies as they continue to pursue the unrealistic goals. This only aggravates their frustration. On the other hand, in a similar situation, the winners face adversity with courage and look for perceptual alternatives. They are clever enough to make constructive use of these released energies to other achievable goals. As a result they reap abundant success. Their secret is in their ability to harness and make best use of the released energies; which otherwise go waste. The trick is in channelling the released energies to achievable realistic goals. Every person who learns this trick can achieve great success. This will surely help you recover from setbacks in previous attempts.

It is important to remember that your instinct to survive will make you resilient, come what may.

Look for opportunities even in the adversity of shattered dreams

Sometimes our dreams get shattered, plans thrown to the winds, hard work and great effort end up in a fiasco. But we must recognise the fact that it is impossible to have a challenge without problems. It may take some time to realise that every problem is an opportunity in disguise. " Opportuniy: it comes disguised in the form of misfortune or temporary defeat," says Success Guru Napoleon Hill. If you can't see it, don't worry, some one will find it.

Many opportunities originate in crisis situations. Look for invisible opportunities in your misfortune. "Small opportunities are often the beginning of great enterprises," says Greek philosopher Demesthenes. Yes, by capturing small opportunities in his life time, Dhirubhai Ambani built the multi-billion dollar Reliance Industries from the scratch. He says, "In every adversity there is an opportunity. If you can read it, you can do it." Yes, you know there are many people in the world who succeeded in life by capturing opportunities. Why not you?

Make the best use of watershed events

"People need trouble, a little bit of frustration to sharpen the spirit on, toughen it," says Nobel laureate William Faulkner. No man is truly tested until adversity has knocked his door. Any fool can remain cheerful when all is well in his world. Yes, it's a shallow life that does not give a person a few scars. Small battles lost should not dilute hopes of victory in war. Be determined to give a brave fight back till the end. No endeavour for success in life should come to an end until the last flame of energy is exhausted.

When driven over to the edge, it is not a good strategy to wait for favourable circumstances. "The only thing that comes to those who wait is whiskers," says an old saying. Remember, unless you take initiative, nobody is going to come to your rescue. Since it is your life at stake, you have to take responsibility and set it right. See past the current difficulties and try to find a way to a happy come back. Remember, the people who get on in this world are the people who get up and look for circumstances they want; and if they can't find them, they make them.

Professors Robert and Jeanette Lauer of the US International University in San Diego, California interviewed 632 people who were able to turn adversity into opportunity. They discovered that most of them made use of a 'watershed event'—a turning point in life—to their advantage. It can be any event, positive or negative, that significantly affects the course of a person's life. They suggest four strategies for mastering life's most unpredictable moments and transforming them into opportunities:

- *Assume responsibility for yourself.* Disappointments are common. "It is important, then to deal actively with painful experiences such as illness, divorce or loss of job," say Lauer and Lauer. "Some people cope by blaming God, fate, or others. But the simple truth is: ultimately we have to assume responsibility for ourselves." Go beyond the hurt and assume responsibility for your life, and make something out of it.
- *Make tough choices..* Try new and tough options in life; they can provide growth. Take risk; it can reward you immensely.
- *Seek relationships that enrich your life.* Relationships are the web of life. They influence how we think. Take help from well-wishing persons. They can instill inspiration and courage at a time we require them most. An experienced mentor could be helpful in providing candid advice, constant encouragement, and continuous support. He can give

tremendous boost to your self-confidence and help you bounce back.
- *Affirm self-worth.* Typically a crisis undermines one's self-esteem, which in turn, makes it difficult to deal with the crisis. "We found that those who were able to affirm a sense of self-worth were less likely to feel helpless and more likely to influence events—and explore options–when faced with adversity," say Lauer and Lauer. Self-esteem is the key to your success.

How this writer bounced back from failure

If you want an authentic story, credible enough to listen, allow me to tell you my real life exposure to failure and how I bounced back to success. If you've never failed in life, this story may not be interesting. Besides, there is every possibility that it may sound like self-bragging. Well, the choice is yours, skip or read:

> My first encounter with failure was my debacle in intermediate examination. I failed with dismal marks in mathematics. When I gave another attempt in the following March, I was crushed again miserably as if under the wheels of a juggernaut. Ever since numbers used to scare me, and higher mathematics frightened me.
>
> My first experience of success was when I passed the clerical grade examination of South Eastern Railway. Way back in 1957, while working in Bilaspur (Chattisgarh), I observed my room-mates busy collecting clippings from newspapers. They were seriously preparing for the Civil Service Examination of the Union Public Service Commission. "If a clerk like me could do it, why not me?" was my immediate reaction. But I felt foolish inside because I was not even a graduate then (hold your smile). I was wondering what talents do they possess that I lack and what more they can do that I cannot do better. I realised that intelligence in itself is not enough to achieve things; there must be something more to

it. I learnt from my friends that the key to success is in systematic preparation and hard work. May be that is what I have to do before I venture to fight with my bugbear—the intermediate exam. Yes, my determination to bounce back from failure is now firmly planted in my brain!

When I was selected as a sorter in Railway Mail Service in my home town Vijayawada (A.P), I felt very happy. But after training, I was a bit disappointed because I was posted at a distant town, Vizianagaram. The job involved sorting letters in a running train; a three-day trip to Vijayawada and back. I was off-duty for three days, and this was the routine. But what to do with free time? Then, it occurred to me: why not do something about the intermediate exam! As the spirit of determination took over, I got down to work.

I collected university question papers in mathematics, physics and chemistry for the last five years, and picked up the stock questions that generally repeated. Prepared thoroughly for all the questions. Learnt every theorem in mathematics, skipped problems though. Memorised answers and practised writing fast without mistakes. Worked hard and spent all the available time for studies. When the results were announced, I was so much shaken by fear of failure and hope of success that I did hesitate to look into the newspaper myself. Seeing my anxiety, someone searched and found my number in the pass list. It was indeed a grand news for anyone who failed once—particularly me. Immediately a great feeling of elation overwhelmed me, because I cleared the biggest hurdle in my life. I felt like the mythical bird phoenix that burnt itself and rose from ashes, young and dynamic once again. My inner voice told me , "if you have done it, you can do anything in this world!" The spirit of the newly discovered self-confidence prompted me to seek higher goals in life.

I became jubilant when I was posted to Vijayawada after two years, but a bit unhappy about night duties. One day I noticed the silver lining of an opportunity, when I saw a colleague attending college during day. Yes, why not me? I joined degree classes in a local college; attended classes in my free time and studied for two years. When the B.A. results were announced, I thought I failed again because I couldn't find my number in the newspaper. Later someone pointed out my mistake. All the while, I was looking in the pass class; whereas it was printed clearly in the second class. This gave me a great relief. Later my professor informed me that I scored the highest marks in the university! It was indeed a great surprise for everybody, including me. Here again my meticulous preparation did the trick, though I did not know how hard I worked.

My renewed confidence once again whispered, "if you could do it with a degree, why not M.A.?" Immediately, I joined the postgraduate course in psychology in Sri Venkateswara University, Tirupati (AP). My kind boss transferred me to nearby Renigunta, where I did my night duties. Every day I used to shuttle the distance to and fro on my bicycle and attended university college during my free time. Striking a balance between night duties and college studies, it was really a strenuous and nerve-wracking struggle for two years. But I thoroughly enjoyed every moment of my endeavour. The grip of determination and the grit of hard work sustained my efforts. And the final result was not that bad—a first class with second rank.

Soon I joined Defence Science Service and had a wonderful time at New Delhi. When I was promoted as a psychologist (a Class I gazetted post) on 33 Services Selection Board, Jabalpur, I had mixed feelings because I felt deprived of the opportunities in the capital city. A surprising element of my new job was that I was required to attend office from 8 am. to 2 pm. Here again I saw an opportunity to continue my studies. I registered for PhD in the local university. One day I saw my neighbour attending Law College in the evening from 6 pm. to 9 pm. Why not me? In three years time I acquired a degree in law; and two years later a doctorate in psychology! It was indeed a dream come true. At that moment an awesome feeling of ecstasy seized my inner soul that evoked a sense of fulfillment; because I achieved an important goal in my life. Unconsciously my lips repeated the famous words: "It is accomplished!"

This is only one side my bounce-back-story. I don't know how it had influenced other people around. At least for my family, it has many positive effects and joyful consequences. Following footsteps, my children made me proud. All the three excelled in studies, and are well settled in US.

Every now and then my eyes get wet when I relive those painful and agonising moments, which I had endured while giving shape to my dreams. Now I feel proud of my painstaking hard work. Yes, overcoming obstacles, bouncing back from failure, emerging on top, is not an easy task; I have experienced it in my own life how arduous it is. Let me tell you my friend, joy is hidden in the struggle for success; it is in the course of seeing through the difficulties that we enjoy the sweetest moments of life. I still wonder how deep is the meaning in the words of General George S. Patton: "Success is how high you bounce when you hit the bottom."

It was my strong determination and persistent effort that helped me to rebound in my life. I realised how right was Calvin Coolidge, a former US President who says: "Nothing in the world can take the place of persistence. Talent will not, nothing is more common than unsuccessful men with talent. Genius will not, unrewarded genius is almost a proverb. Education will not, the world is full of educated failures. Persistence and determination alone are important." Yes, success cannot but yield to perseverance and persistence. When you bounce back in life the turnaround success will give so much confidence that will make you think of unlimited possibilities.

You are welcome my friend, if you like to draw a bit of inspiration from this humble story. If a little soul like me could do it, can't you? Think about it, do something remarkable in life. Believe me, you can do it! If you want further motivation, read Billi PS Lim's interesting book *Dare to Fail*. His major mascot is the bounce back doll. Just as the doll is knocked down to the ground and rebounds back, Lim feels only a failed person has what it takes to achieve success!

Relish the sweet honey of your small achievements

All of us have a lot of achievements to our credit, as well as failures. Yet, we often ponder over the failures unhappily, ignoring the triumphs that are so dear to us. Why not we bring to our mind our successful achievements to cement our feelings of self-confidence? When you have a glass of milk right in your hand, why cry over a few drops of spilt milk? Doesn't it look funny? Do you know what the spilt milk contains—your lost opportunities, failures, disappointments, frustrations, unhappy feelings." It is not what we have lost that's important," says famous South African heart surgeon Christiaan N. Barnard. "What is important is what you have." Forget what you have lost. Remember, happiness is not wishing for what we don't have but enjoying what we have. Learn to relish the sweet honey of your own achievements, however small they are: Your academic achievements, degrees acquired, your professional triumphs, success of the assignments handled, business success, the money you have made, the house or flat you have acquired, the car you have purchased, accomplished children you brought up, your style of living, and your creative achievements—excellent hand work you have done, your paintings, your poetry, etc.

It is not necessary that you should wait for big achievements to reminisce and enjoy. Remember, no goal is too insignificant if it contributes to your sense of well-being! Even the small things have the potential to offer pleasure and joy: a dress you made for your baby, a toy you made for your son, a neatly kept house, a work done well, a beautiful drawing, a well-written letter, a beautiful sentence you wrote, the "thank you" letter you sent to a friend, flowers and vegetables you have grown in your garden, a tasty new dish you have made, a small gift you have given to a poor child. These are small achievements, no doubt; but they deserve to be appreciated, admired, and enjoyed. Every time you remember them, the joyful feelings of these small successes will overwhelm you, infusing new strengths to your self-esteem and confidence. They will rejuvenate you with the happy-to-be-alive attitudes. "Life is made up of small pleasures," says American writer Norman Lear. " Happiness is made up of those tiny successes. The big ones come too infrequently. And if you don't collect all these tiny successes, the big ones don't really mean anything." Small successes are indeed the building blocks of a joyful life!

Don't get distracted by success

Joy of success disappears when your mind is distracted. " Once a person becomes famous a bunch of sycophants automatically try to gather around him" says Geet Sethi, seven times World Billiards Champion. " Their adulation can go to a person's head and blind him to reality."

Sethi observed that his world changed after his success caused distress. "I was no longer enjoying myself. My life had become an intricate web of distractions with me firmly trapped in the middle. These self-destructive distractions ranged from wanting to build a house , to wanting to establish business, wanting to make money and so many other desires." Beyond this was something worse, "But the unkindest cut of all was that everyone was talking about my success, not my joy," he says ruefully. His simple tip is to design a life style not cluttered, but focus on the activities of your interest and family.

Forget success and failure: pursue your own way
In 1930, a letter from England posed the following question to Nobel laureate Albert Einstein: "If, on your death bed, you looked back on your life, by what facts would you determine whether it was a success or failure?" "Neither on my death bed nor before will I ask myself such a question. Nature is not an engineer or contractor, and I myself am a part of nature," (*Reader's Digest*, Oct. '79). In another context he says, "Try not to become a man of success. Rather, become a man of value." Dag Hammarskjold, the late UN Secretary General once wrote, " a successful life is doubly a lie; an error which has to be corrected, is a heavier burden than truth."

All sports persons know that winning and losing is part of the game; and the real joy is in playing. In the same way many sensible people know that success and failure are part of life; and beyond winning and losing, they realise that what's important is how we enjoy while playing our role in the drama called 'life.' And the real joy is in the struggle to achieve something before we end this mortal life.

"It is not necessary that every person should strive to achieve success in life," says American naturalist Henry David Thoreau. "I would have each one be very careful to find out and pursue his own way. Let everyone mind his own business, and endeavour to be what he was made. Why should we be in such a desperate haste to succeed and in such desperate enterprises? If a man does not keep pace with his companions, perhaps it is because he hears a different drummer. Let him step to the music he hears, however measured or far away." He says that every person is free to choose his own way of living. As American writer Christopher Morley puts it, "There is only one success—to be able to spend your life in your own way."

Remember, the joy of success is relative

Gururj Deshpande, a self-made technocrat-entrepreneur who built the billion dollar Sycamore Networks (US), once narrated the following to tell us how relative is success:

"At age 4 success is .. not peeing in the pants.
.. 16 .. .. .. having a driver's license.
.. 20 .. .. .. having sex.
.. 35 .. .. .. having a good job.
.. 55 .. .. .. having money.
.. 70 .. .. .. having sex.
.. 80 .. .. .. having a driver's license.
.. 90 .. .. .. not peeing in the pants.

With due apologies to all my friends over age 70, success is after all a relative term." At the end, Deshpande made a profound statement: "Success is being at peace with yourself."

Be Happy: Living Is Joy Enough

It is not the level of prosperity that makes for happiness but the kinship of heart to heart and the way we look at the world. Both attributes are within our power, so that a man is happy so long as he chooses to be happy; and no one can stop him.

Aleksander Solzhenytsyn (b.1918-)
Russian Author, Historian, Nobel Prize 1970

Be happy: it is a way of being wise.

Colette (Sidonie Gabrielle Claude) (1873-1954)
French Novelist

Happiness is the very purpose of life

"It is a sorry business that God has given man to busy himself with. I have seen all the deeds that are done under the sun. They are all emptiness, and chasing the wind. I know there is nothing good for man except to be happy and live the best life he can while he is alive," says the wise King Solomon. Yes, there is nothing greater in life than seeking happiness and fulfilment. According to Greek philosopher Aristotle, "Happiness is the meaning and purpose of life, the whole aim and end of human existence."

"How to gain, how to keep, how to recover happiness is, in fact for most men at all times the secret motive of what all they do, and all they are willing to endure," points out American author Dean William Randolph Inge. Let us begin from the recognition that all human beings cherish happiness and do not want suffering.

So, let us focus on the urgent desire of our times by exploring happiness with extraordinary exuberance.

Happiness is a universal right

"Happiness is a birthright," says American poet Ella Wheeler Wilcox. "No matter how dull, or how mean, how wise a man is, he feels that happiness is his indisputable birthright. Right to happiness is fundamental," says Helen Keller, the born blind, dumb and deaf. Be it right to wealth or right to happiness, benefits accrue only when the right is exercised. Yes, we have every right to exercise this right to happiness for our benefit. It requires inner desire and conscious effort on our part to enjoy what life offers.

Manu Smrithi, a treatise on ancient Indian law, recognises the universal "right to happiness." Life, liberty and pursuit of happiness are ordained in the American Constitution. American Statesman Benjamin Franklin warns, "The Constitution only guarantees the right to happiness. You have to catch it yourself."

"The best public policy is that which produces the greatest happiness," says Jeremy Bentham, well known British economist. A similar argument is put forward by a modern Economist Richard Layard in his recent book, *Happiness: Lessons from a New Science.* According to him public policy should be devoted to increasing happiness rather than wealth or success. Many economists argue that happiness is not just a state of mind, it should be a policy for the government. They call for political reforms that would increase the happiness of the average person. Thus, the latest thinking among economists is that happiness is the ultimate goal for society.

During the 90's economists all over the world advocated a broader approach to improving human well-being. They emphasised the need to put people, their needs, their aspirations and their capabilities at the centre of the developmental effort. Later some economists have realised that Gross National Product (GDP) is not a good indicator of the quality of life. Several countries are concerned about the Human Development Index (HDI) ranking and are trying to measure the standard of living through alternative models.

They have been shifting their emphasis from GDP to Genuine Progressive Indicator (GPI) developed by a US-based organisation, Redefining Progress. This model adjusts the GDP for 10 indicators such as pollution and non-monetary work of home makers. It classifies expenditures of time and money as positive or negative to estimate economic well-being. Some say it is not adequate to measure the real well-being. The latest thinking is reflected in the term, Gross National Happiness (GNH) that redefines human well-being. The government of Bhutan thought it fit to embrace this concept and adopted it as its national policy. At its core, the GNH is a civilised vision anchored in non-material values such as living in harmony with nature, social equality and spiritual quest for higher levels of being.

Happiness is subjective

For the Arabian poet Omar Khayyam, happiness is a piece of bread, a cup of wine, a good book, and his lady love beside. Jean Jacques Rousseau, a French philosopher says, "Happiness is a good bank account, a good cook and good digestion." Former US President Franklin D. Roosevelt says, "Happiness is not in the possession of money, it is in the joy of achievement, and in the thrill of creative effort." A well-known British philosopher Betrand Russell says, "A happy life must be to a great extent a quiet life, for it is only in the atmosphere of quiet that true joy can live." In all these statements, happiness differs from person to person. The undertone indicates the *subjective* nature of happiness. What makes you happy depends absolutely on your notion of happiness.

Happiness is a never-found-land
Everybody can feel happy; but nobody can reach the never-found-land of happiness. Simply because happiness is an awesome concept conceived by mind that lies within; it does not exist anywhere else. That's the truth about happiness. "Your success and happiness lie within you," says Helen Keller, "External conditions are the accidents of life, its outer trappings." An English man of letters Sir Roger L'Estrange says, " It is not the place, nor the condition, but the mind alone, that can make anyone happy or miserable." It is up to you to choose between happiness and unhappiness. Psychotherapist Bill Little says ,"(Un)happiness is something you choose" (*Reader's Digest*, April '82).

Success and happiness are states of mind. Real happiness comes from within. Nobody can give it to you. In "One Sure Way to Happiness" (*Reader's Digest*, Jan."65), American author June Callwood says, "Happiness is the rarest, and most prized and misunderstood state of man. Actually, lasting happiness depends on how much maturity a man has been able to assemble –some of it derived from being desperately unhappy. It is a consequence of at least a moderate amount of education or training, because happiness requires a decently stocked mind. It is bound up with the ability to work and to be readily interested in the world around you."

Pursuit of happiness is like chasing the wind
"The thirst for happiness is never extinguished in the heart of man," says French philosopher Jean Jacques Rousseau. Yes, the quest for happiness is never ending. The more one chases it , the more elusive it remains. Running after the intangible happiness is like chasing the wind. It is difficult to comprehend happiness, though it exists in our feelings.

American poet Priscilla Leonard describes the abstract nature of happiness in the following poem:

> Happiness is like a crystal
> Fair and exquisite and clear,
> Broken in a million pieces,
> Shattered, scattered, far and near.
>
> Now and then along life's pathway,
> Lo ! Some shining fragments fall;
> But there are so many pieces
> None ever finds them all.
>
> You may find a bit of beauty,
> Or an honest share of wealth,
> While another, just beside you
> Gathers honour, love, or health.
>
> Vain to choose or grasp unduly,
> Broken is the perfect ball;
> And there are so many pieces,
> None finds them all.
>
> Yet the wise, as on their journey
> Treasure every fragment clear,
> Fit them as they may together ,
> Imagining the shattered sphere.
>
> Learning ever to be thankful,
> Though their share of it is small:
> For it has so many pieces
> None finds them all.

Yes, happiness is a subtle concept, abstract in nature. But many people assume its existence. "Most people are searching for happiness," says Psychotherapist Wayne Dyer. They are looking for it. They try to find it in someone or something outside of themselves. This is a fundamental mistake. Happiness is something that you are, and it comes from the way you think.

Therefore it is not wise to view success or happiness as life-goals. Pursuing happiness would be like chasing the wind. When you do that it looks " untextured, toothless, bleached of nuance and subtlety," says American author Ziyad Marar in *Happiness Paradox*. But when you pursue your goals you will discover that the happiness comes along. There is no such thing as the pursuit of happiness, but there is the discovery of joy.

Happiness is conditioned in adults

"Man is born free but everywhere he is in chains," says a French philosopher Jean Jacques Rousseu. Yes, we are originally designed to feel free to be happy. Infants and children demonstrate this fact in as much as they feel happy without any preconditions. As children we used to express happiness very freely. But in our upbringing we are gradually conditioned. Only when we grew up we learned our self-defeating behaviour. We condition ourselves by saying, "If I get this I will be *happy* or if I don't get that I will be damn *unhappy*." People associate happiness with the occurrence of an event. As Composer Arthur Rubinstein points out, "Most people ask for happiness on condition. Happiness can only be felt if you don't set any condition."

The Nobel Prize winning Russian physiologist Ivan Pavlov was the first to use the terms "conditioning" and "de-conditioning" and "conditioned reflexes." According to him we can learn to de-condition our habitual responses to external stimuli. We have the ability to feel happy whenever we want, if only we get rid of the conditioned stimuli that are chained to our feelings. Make effort to get rid of those chains of habit. You have nothing to lose but your chains. We can de-condition socially desirable things and events that were linked to our happiness. And we can condition our happiness to our own small achievements. If we can do this, our actions do not require approval from others. Nobody can stop you feeling what you want to feel. Then, whatever we do will be the source of joy. The choice is yours. It is all up to you. If you really want to feel happy, nobody can stop you. Do not set any conditions for your happiness. Russian author Leo Tolstoy says, "If you want to be happy, be."

Happiness as a by-product

Happiness is such a fluid, shifting, fleeting, dynamic state, that you are always surprised by joy. You may try to lay hold of it—through music, through work, through sport, through sex—happiness always comes to you as a side-effect of other pursuits. As American physician Dr Benjamin Spok says, "Happiness is mostly a by-product of doing what makes us feel fulfilled."

Yes, happiness comes as a by-product of some action or effort. As American author James Muriel says, "Most of us experience happiness when we are enjoying life and feeling free, enjoying the process and the products of our intellectual and processes, enjoying the transcendent oneness with the universe."

Happiness always comes not as an end in itself but as a side-effect of other pursuits. Though we may think of happiness as our life-goal, we need something else that produces happiness in us. In the recent novel *Saturday*, Ian McEwan narrates why happiness is all important, and why we never isolate it from all our desires. American writer Natasha Walter points out that "Happiness may now be the current goal of our lives, we need those old ideals—if not religion, say justice, or freedom, or love—to show us the way,"

Happiness is a joy mingled with pleasure

Pleasure is indeed another form of happiness. Our senses afford us to enjoy many pleasures such as beautiful pieces of art, melodious music, fragrant flowers, delicious food, etc. And the sensual pleasures of our body are numerous, such as a pleasant touch, a sweet kiss, and thrilling sex. " Pleasure is the freedom song, but is not the freedom. It is the blossoming of desires, but it is not the fruit," says Lebanese philosopher Kahlil Gibran. Our happiness is made up of happy feelings; they are mingled with the pleasure and joy we experience.

Pleasures vs gratifications (enjoyments)

"Happiness in the present moment consists of very different states of happiness about the past or future. It embraces two different kinds of things: pleasures and gratifications," says Psychologist Martin E.P. Seligman of the University of Pennsylvania. "The pleasures are delights that have clear sensory and strong emotional components; what philosophers call raw "feels": ecstasy, thrills, orgasm, delight, mirth, exuberance and comfort." Pleasures are evanescent and they involve little, if any, thinking. Bodily pleasures are delights that are immediate, come through the senses and are momentary. Pleasures are shortcuts to happiness and are short lived. Philosopher George Santayana says, " A string of excited, fugitive, miscellaneous pleasures is not happiness." American author Josh Billings says, "Don't mistake pleasure for happiness. They are a different breed of dogs."

On the other hand the gratifications are activities, we very much like doing, but they are not necessarily accompanied by any raw feelings at all. In contrast to pleasures, where getting in touch with feelings is important, the defining criterion for gratification is the absence of feeling, loss of consciousness, and total engagement. The gratifications engage us fully, we become immersed and absorbed in them, we lose self-consciousness. Enjoying a great conversation, rock climbing, reading a good book, dancing are all examples of activities, in which time stops for us, our skills match the challenge, and we are in touch with our (signature) strengths—intelligence, creative abilities, talents, special skills. They involve a lot of thinking and interpretation. They do not habituate easily (unlike pleasures), and they are undergirded by our strengths and virtues. The joy we get from gratifications lasts longer than pleasures.

A little pleasure is not that bad
"Where your pleasure is, there is your treasure; where your treasure, there your heart, where your heart, there your happiness," says St. Augustine. "Is there something out there, some lost key to the kingdom of happiness, that is being overlooked?" asks Michael Flocker in *The Hedonism Handbook*. " It is called pleasure," he answers emphatically. Yes, this view shatters our age-old conviction that an overdose of pleasurable things will spoil our lives. We cannot but agree with his views: "A life lived without pleasure, beauty and a sensible degree of self-indulgence is a sad and wasted one."

Psycho-cybernetics guru Maxwell Maltz says:

"Living should be a happy vocation," People should be useful to themselves and others. Pleasure must be part of us –like our heart, our eyes, our hands, our feet. It should know no race, no creed, no colour, no status, no age. The good feelings in life belong to us and there is no moral aspect to it except that it is immoral for people to fester in unhappiness."

"Give yourself the right to be happy. You must give yourself this right at any age. Stop shortchanging yourself; stop blocking your pleasure. The "pursuit of pleasure" is your human right.... Court pleasure, not pain. Pay homage to its virtues; feel that you are worthy. Find pleasure in the little things, food that tastes delicious, friendship that is sincere, a sun that is warming, a smile that is meant to cheer."

But overindulgence may cause depression
The philosophy of pleasure appeals to youth because they are passing through a phase of life that looks for immediate joys and

pleasures; they don't even bother to abide by the restrictions of the society. "Most men pursue pleasure in such breathless haste that they hurry past it," says American author Soren Kirkegaard. The pleasures they crave for have a tendency to make them addictive. The hallmark of addictive pleasures is that more and more is needed to reach the initial level of satisfaction. And this craving can enslave an individual. Philosophers advise us to get detached from addictive things, but not with simple pleasures. Enjoy the pleasures but overcome dependence. If you cannot renounce dependence, the genius of pleasure will never salute you. A bit of pleasure is always desirable but steer clear of excessive indulgence.

Professor Seligman says, "Over reliance on shortcuts to happiness may be the cause of the modern epidemic of depression. These shortcuts require no skill, no effort. What would happen if my entire life were made up of such easy pleasures, never calling on my strengths, never presenting challenges? Such a life sets me for depression. The strengths and virtues may wither during the life of taking shortcuts rather than choosing a life made full through the pursuit of gratifications."

Lasting joy comes from gratifications

Lasting joy comes from turning away from lower pleasures and seeking the higher ones. " The pleasant things in the world are pleasant thoughts; and the great art of life is to have as many of them as possible," says French author Michael de Montaigne. "Pleasure is a powerful source of motivation, but it does not produce challenge; it is a conservative force that makes us want to satisfy existing needs, achieve comfort and relaxation," says Psychologist Mihaly Csikszentmihalyi (pronounced 'cheeks sent me high'). "Enjoyment (gratification) on the other hand is not always present, and it can be utterly stressful at times. A mountain climber may be close to freezing, utterly exhausted, in danger of falling into bottomless crevasse, yet wouldn't want to be anywhere else. Sipping a cocktail under a palm tree at the edge of turquoise ocean is nice, but it just doesn't compare to the exhilaration he feels on the freezing ridge."

The gratifications produce *flow*—a joyful feeling, but they require skill and effort; even more deterring is the fact that because they meet the challenges, they offer the possibility of failing. Engaging in gratifying tasks (e.g.. playing three sets of tennis, participating in a clever conversation, reading Richard Russo) takes work —at least to start with. The pleasures do not: watching TV, masturbating, inhaling perfume are not challenging. Eating a buttered bagel, or viewing a televised football on Monday night requires no skill, no effort, and there is no possibility of failures.

"The question of enhancing gratifications is nothing less than and nothing more than the venerable question: 'What is the good life?' "says Seligman. "The belief that we can rely on shortcuts to gratification and bypass the exercise of personal strengths and virtues is folly. It leads to legions of humanity who are depressed in the middle of great wealth and starving to death spiritually. Such people ask, "How can I be happy?" This is the wrong question, because without the distinction between pleasure and gratification, it leads all easily to total reliance on shortcuts, to a life of snatching up as many easy pleasures as possible.

Gratifications last long unlike short-lived pleasures. They are our psychological capital. When we engage in pleasures, we are just consuming. The smell of perfume, taste of raspberries, sensitivity of a scalp rub or massage are all momentary delights, but they do not do anything for the future. They are not investments, nothing is accumulated for the future.

When we are engaged in gratifications (or absorbed in flow), perhaps we are investing, building psychological capital for the future. Perhaps the flow is the state that marks growth.

Absorption, the loss of consciousness, and stopping time may be evolution's way of telling us that we are stocking up reserves for the future. In this analogy, pleasure marks the achievement of biological satiation, whereas gratification marks the achievement of growth. American author Lawana Blackwell says, "I have grown to realise that the joy that comes from little victories is preferable to the fun that comes from ease and pursuit of pleasure."

Starting the process of eschewing easy pleasures and engaging in more gratifications is hard. Gratification dispels self-absorption, the more one has the *flow* that gratification produces, the less depressed one is. Here then is a powerful antidote to the epidemic of depression in youth. Seligman says, "Strive for more gratifications while toning down the pursuit of pleasure. The pleasures come easily, and the gratifications (which come from the exercise of personal strengths) are hard-won."

Happiness improves health, increases longevity

Positive emotions have a profound purpose beyond the delightful way they make us feel. When we are in a positive mood people like us better and friendship, love, coalitions are more likely to cement. In contrast to the constrictions of negative emotions, our mindset is expansive, tolerant and creative. We are open to new ideas and new experiences.

Psychologists have identified at least three positive emotions – joy, interest, and contentment. Professor Barbara Frederickson of the University of Michigan points out that not only do joy, interest and contentment share the feature of broadening an individual's momentary thought–action repertoire but they also share the feature of building resources ranging from physical, intellectual and social resources. Importantly these resources are more durable than the transient emotional states that led to their acquisition. By consequence, then, the often incidental effect of experiencing a positive emotion is an increment in enduring personal resources that can be drawn later, in other contexts, in other emotional states. She says that cultivation of these positive emotional states optimise health and well-being.

People who are happy in their daily lives have healthier levels of vital body chemicals than those who get few positive feelings, according to a recent study reported in *New Scientist*. The research at London University College has linked everyday happiness with healthier levels of important body chemicals. This means happier people have healthier hearts and cardiovascular systems, and possibly less prone to diseases like diabetes.

"Happiness is not transitory joy but longevity of secret power," says German philosopher Johaan Wolfgang Von Goethe. People do believe that happiness leads to good health and longevity. Recently scientists have uncovered the link between the state of mind and long-term health. Professor Andrew Steptoe and his colleagues at University College London asked 200 middle-aged civil servants how many happy moments they experienced during a typical day. The happiest people had lower levels of chemicals which are linked to heart disease and Type II diabetes. Steptoe adds: "It has been suspected for the last few years that happier people may be healthier, both mentally and physically, than less healthy people. What this study shows is that there are plausible biological pathways linking happiness with health."

The researchers monitored the emotional and physical state of the volunteers at work, at home and in the laboratory. They found that the saliva of those who were the happiest had lower levels of cortisol, a stress hormone related to conditions including type II diabetes and high blood pressure. Happier men had significantly lower heart rates—down from 76 beats a minute to 68-70. Men and women who were generally unhappy reacted to stress by producing more plasma fibrinogen chemicals in their blood—a strong predictor of cardiovascular disease. These scientists say that a happy worker is a healthy worker.

It is wise to be happy

"Be happy: It is a way of being wise," says French writer Colette. It is indeed a profound message. The messages that follow are equally insightful. Read what the wise people say:

"Happiness is the proof of success in the art of living."
Eric Fromm, Austrian psychiatrist

"Happiness is a gift you give it yourself—not just during Christmas, but all year round…To live creatively *you* must allow *yourself* happiness. *You.* You must do it. Your self image.. Your self image must be strong enough so that you sustain this feeling of pleasure."
Maxwell Maltz, Psycho-cybernetics guru

"It is good to be just plain happy, it's a little better to know you're happy. But to understand that you're happy and know how and why…and still be happy in the being and knowing, well that is beyond happiness, that is bliss."
Henry Miller, American author

"Humanity does not want us to be happy. It merely asks us to be brilliant on its behalf—survival first, then happiness as we can manage it."
Orson Scott Card, American writer

"Switch on your life and ground yourself in happiness!"
Hugh Prather, American counselor

"Do what must be done. This may not be happiness, but it is greatness."
George Bernard Shaw, Nobel laureate

"Act happy, feel happy, be happy without a reason in the world. Then you can love, and do what you will."
Don Millman, American author

11

Keep Happy Memories Alive: Create Your Own Paradise

> The time present is seldom able to fill desire or imagination with immediate enjoyment, and we are forced to supply its deficiencies by recollection or anticipation.
>
> *Samuel Johnson (1709-1784)*
> English poet, essayist, critic

> A memory may be a paradise from which we cannot be driven. It may also be a hell from which we cannot escape.
>
> *John Lancaster Spalding (1840-1916)*
> Archbishop of Scintopolis, US.

Past memories always find a way of coming back
"Incidence of memory is like the light from the dead stars whose influence lingers long after the events themselves," says American author David Horowitz. Our past memories always come back. Nobody is in a position to stop them. Professor Peter Berger tells us the unforgettable truth about our past: "Past is malleable and flexible, changing as our reflection interprets and re-explains what has happened." Our past is like a kaleidoscope; every time we tilt it, its colourful reflections change. Every time our mind re-examines the memories, our interpretations take on different meanings. That is the inevitable problem with our memory.

Our past is an assortment of all sorts of things—good and bad, beautiful and ugly, and joyful and sorrowful. But we are often perturbed by the unhappy memories, while forgetting joyful events. Many wise people say that the only remedy is to forget the past. Alexander MacLaren, a British preacher, says, "Forget your past circumstances whether they be sorrows or joys. The one is not without remedy, the other not perfect. Both are past, why remember them. Why should you carry about parched corn when you dwell among fields white unto harvest? Why carry putrid water in the bottom of a rancid skin, when living in a land of fountains and brooks that run among hills? Why clasp a handful of withered flowers, when the grass is shown with their bright eyes opening to the sunshine." 'Forget the past and live in the present' seems to be a good piece of advice. But forgetting the past with all its joys and sorrows is like throwing the baby with the bath water.

We all look for joy in our lives and try to enjoy every moment. But sometimes the present moment does not offer joy, as it is dull and drab. We try to solve this problem by seeking escape. British author Samuel Johnson observes: "The time present is seldom able to fill desire or imagination with immediate enjoyment, and we are forced to supply its deficiencies by recollection or anticipation." Yes, we fill the dull moments either by recalling joyful moments in the past or dreaming and enjoying the fantasies about future. This is a natural gift we all have. Yes, we are gifted with the power to forget what is painful and recall what is joyful when we are bored with the present. This is a great blessing and solace, because we can remember joyful experiences and enjoy them whenever we want. When we do this, the bitterness of unpleasant feelings fades away as they are out of focus.

Life being a series of problems, we cannot survive without drawing from our inner resources—our learning experiences and joyful memories in particular. We can recall them and apply them in handling current problems here and now. Learning from past experiences brings hope, confidence and renewal in our lives. When the present does not offer joy we can always resort to recalling happy memories. That ensures continuous flow of joy in our lives. That is where our mind comes to our rescue releasing great energies to uplift us with abundant joy all through the twists and turns of life.

Then why not make a deliberate attempt, to create a paradise here and now with the solid bricks of your joyful memories? Yes, when dull moments threaten to bore us we can always choose to enjoy a short sojourn in our heavenly abode.

Recall happy memories: create your own paradise

"Insufficient appreciation and savouring of good events in your past and overemphasis of bad ones are the true culprits that undermine serenity, contentment, and satisfaction," says Psychologist Martin E.P. Seligman of the University of Pennsylvania. True, if we can recall joyful memories every time we have sad thoughts, the effect will be marvellous. It works like a magic wand that transforms depressing thoughts into heavenly moments. If you can recall and appreciate good things in life, you can relive those happy moments and enjoy them once again.

"Happy experiences give us lovely memories to warm the history of our lives," says American author Ardis Whitman. "Each happiness of yesterday is a pleasant memory for today." Happy times are never gone as long as pleasant memories are stored in the brain. Happy memories spring up most readily to mind whenever we recall them. Since they never fade out, you can remember them as often as you want. It is hard to resist remembering joyful events in life. Always remember the joyful moments that made you happy, and forget things that made you sad. Recalling sweet memories is the best course when the present moment is dull and drab.

If you really want to boost your happiness, take a fascinating trip down the memory lane and bring back all the good things that life has showered upon you. Relive those good old times that you enjoyed in life: the innocent days of childhood, the make-believe games you played and enjoyed; the fantastic world of your adolescence, and your innocent search for love in every soul around, the love songs that you sang and the music you enjoyed; your yearning for the love of the opposite sex; bubbling energy of youthful days; your brave attempts and sizzling actions with the urge to accomplish ; and the good tally of not-so-small achievements of yours; the blissful moments you enjoyed with your spouse; joyful days of upbringing children, their marriage and settlement; the joy of seeing grandchildren, dreams of their future; and the finest moments of peace, serenity and tranquillity in the sunset years. Yes, good times last for a lifetime. You can always reminisce and enjoy.

You can create a paradise on earth by recalling happy memories and joyful moments because it is natural for human mind to eliminate unpleasant memories and retain pleasant ones. Surely it will transport your soul to a time zone that transcends your life-time. Get ready to a feast of sweet memories and heavenly moments. You can enjoy and relive those blessed moments of joy and wonder in your life. Visit your virtual paradise whenever you want, and enjoy the exuberance and enchantment of all the blissful moments in life.

Yes, reliving the joyous moments in life is indeed finding heaven on earth. Come, sit back and get nostalgic. Just revel in the rhapsody of happy memories and rediscover your past world of delight. Each moment of ecstasy is draped in joy and laced with pleasure. They will cradle you in the lap of cushioned luxury in the unparalleled ambience of your own paradise with a promise of happiness, peace, serenity and tranquillity. It is always good to have a back-up of joyful memories to fall back upon during unpleasant moments in life. But take note of the warning of Oscar Hammling: "Often the greatest enemy of present happiness is the past happiness too well remembered".

"When I'm sad I simply remember my favourite things," sings actress Julie Andrews. We may like to join her in the chorus, remembering all the joyful things in life. Come, sing along everybody. Let us sing with American comedian Bob Hope, "Thanks for the memory."

Count your blessings when miseries come

In order to be happy now you should forget your unhappy memories. If they keep bothering you, harden your stance and silence them with the help of their enemies—the joyful memories. One way of doing this is to keep a 'Happiness Calendar' suggested by American journalist John Culhane (*Reader's Digest*, June '87). He devised it for organised counting of blessings. He thinks that reminiscing joyful events in life is one way to keep off the inevitable problems in life. It's a wonderful idea worth implementing.

He bought a calendar with big blank squares for every day of the year, and on it began to record when, where and with whom he has been most happy. Based on the daily appointment calendars he has kept for years, this master calendar will eventually register the 365 happiest days of his life.

From the start his method was simple. At the top of his Happiness Calendar, he wrote: " I Count Only the Sunny Days," Then he went on a hunt for happy days through all the journals and engagement calendars, he has kept for a long time. Out of this raw material, he compiled a list of the happiest days of his life, from childhood up to 1982. Then he worked out a simple three-step plan for keeping such a calendar up-to-date.

First, at the end of each month, he will select from current appointment calendar three or four days on which he was happiest. These become headlines at the top of that month's page. Here, for example, are the headlines for January 1982: "Michael and T.H. Play for Holiday Parties." And "Hind and I celebrate Virgil's Birthday." He explains, Michael and T.H.—for Thomas Henry—are his sons and they played their guitars for parties on January 1 and 2. Hind is his wife, and they had a birthday party on January 11 for their friend Virgil Burnett.

Step two takes place on New Year's Day of the following year, when he sorts through the monthly headlines and add their dates to the Happiness Calendar. The third step starts when he has already recorded a happiest day on a certain date. He jots down the new happy day on the back of the calendar. When he completes this happiest year of his life, he will start another one. He says, "After all you can't have too many happier years." Culhane says, Happiness Calendar will help reminiscing joyful events in life, it is one way to keep off the inevitable miseries in life. Here are some of the entries in the Happiness Calendar of this writer to demonstrate how unhappy days are compensated by happy events in life:

The 10th March 1966. "Today, first time in my life, I felt what it is like to be lonely. It is quite unbearable. It is just one minute past 1'o clock a.m. At this hour of silence I do feel I am lonely…same must be the case with my wife…poor girl." This unhappy day is also associated with a happy day in 2005. My diary entry says: "MD of Sterling publishers rang up. Informed me the good news that they have just started the printing process of my new book *Born to be Happy: Enjoy Life to the Full.*"

The 21st April 1964. "Yesterday was the first starving day for all the members of my family. Somehow late in the evening, I brought a few coins from a friend and bought some rice." This gloomy day is also connected with a joyful day in 2005: "Delighted to see a sun-ball flower suddenly sprouting up. We enjoyed its stunning beauty." The green foliage of this plant remains for six months till it stores enough food required for rest of the year. It hibernates for six months, only to shoot up a beautiful flower one fine morning in summer. Nature seems to teach us a lesson through this plant: 'save first, then you can enjoy life.'

The 1st July 1961 was the saddest day in my life. "My mother died on this day. Everyone was crying. Since my father was not available, I had to look after the cremation formalities." But this black day also brings back a happy memory of a wonderful day in 1977, when I enjoyed a lavish function, at East-West Center, Honolulu in connection with my participation in the Research Methodology Workshop on Identification, Selection and, Development of Entrepreneurs.

In the words of Culhane, "Here was a proof that no matter how miserable this day of this month of this year may have been, I had already been happy on this date. And chances are, in some future year this day will be even happier."

"Do not care for the darkest cloudy nights in your life; concentrate on the light of the brilliant stars that will be shedding their light on your path," says an anonymous philosopher. Come on, make a Happiness Calendar of your own. When you bring happy moments into limelight, unhappy memories will fade away like morning mist before the warm sun. Remember, only memories of good times last. Surely, if you relive those happy events of the past, you will enjoy them time and time again. These strings of joyful moments will ultimately add up to make a blissful life. Happiness indeed depends on your ability to count your blessings; and it is in your hands to make a life filled with joy!

Reprogramme your mind to relive happy moments

Your mind is programmed to retrieve everything in your memory! And the most incredible thing is, it can learn what you teach. If you can teach a shift in perception, it will readily recall the happiest moments in life. "Search around in your mind each day for your successful memories—get into the habit of searching for these wonderful moments—and bring these realistically happy times front stage center," says Maxwell Maltz, the Psycho-cybernetics guru. " See yourself this way, successful, acting and thinking the way you like to act and think; reactivate these positive images each day. Not only must you focus on your picture of contentment, but you must also be kind to your areas of weakness if pleasure is to be a factor in your life. This building up of your self-image, make it a daily habit of prime importance; pleasure starts with yourself."

Come create your own paradise. "By heaven we understand that it is a state of happiness infinite in degree and endless in duration," says American Statesman Benjamin Franklin. Yes, if the state of happiness is identified as a heaven, we can create it on earth in our own life of finite duration. That is what you may call a personal paradise, a heaven of your own. We can recall the joyful moments in life with the help of our mind—a friend and life partner. We can summon our pleasant memories, and relive those blissful moments of joy. Remember, the brighter moments of our past can always overshadow the bleak ones in the present. Just sit back, relax, find your own heaven where you are. Now reminisce and enjoy the sweet memories of your proud moments of success and triumph. Meditate on life's ecstasies and relive those joyful moments as often as you can and make a lifetime of happiness!

12
Celebrate the Festival of Life: Enjoy While You Are Alive

> Suddenly I realised .. a profound lesson in getting on with the business of living. Because the business of living is joy in the real sense of the word, not just something for pleasure, amusement, recreation. The business of living is celebration of being alive.
>
> *Christiaan N Barnard* (1922-2001)
> South African heart surgeon

> Enjoy the festival of life with other men.
>
> *Epictetus (55-145 AD)*
> Roman stoic philosopher

You have one time opportunity to live a joyful life
Now is the time to savour finer nuances of life and feel happy and rejoice all the joys it offers. See all things in life as blessings and opportunities to learn, love and enjoy. " Joy is the happiness of love—love is awareness of its own inner happiness," says Bishop Fulton J. Sheen. "Pleasure comes from without, and joy comes from within, and it is therefore within the reach of every one in the world." Joy does not simply happen to us; we have to choose it every day.

"Enjoy yourself and be happy," says Maharshi Mahesh Yogi. "Being happy is of utmost importance. Success in anything is through happiness. More support of nature comes from being happy, even if you have to force it a bit to some long standing habits. Just think of any negativity that comes to you as a raindrop falling into the ocean of your bliss. You may not have an ocean of bliss, think that any way it will help it come. Doubting is not blissful and it does not create happiness. Be happy, healthy and let all that love come through your heart."

Business of living is joy

In "In Celebration of Being Alive" (*Reader's Digest*, Dec '80), Christiaan N. Barnard, the famous South African heart surgeon, describes how he survived a terrible car accident that almost crushed him. It was indeed a great moment of joy for him to know that he was still alive. He wrote, "Suddenly, I realised,… a profound lesson in getting on with the business of living. Because the business of living is joy in the real sense of the word, not just something for pleasure, amusement, recreation. The business of living is the celebration of being alive."

We don't need an accident to realise that we are still alive to enjoy life, though we are certain we don't live for ever. The message is clear: Celebrate, you are still alive!

Joy is everywhere

Nobel laureate Rabindranath Tagore quotes a poem from *Ishopanishat*, in his book *Personality*. The ancient poet sings, "The earth is His joy," and everything here is joyful. Emphasising the same theme, Tagore himself wrote the following poem *Joy*.

> And Joy is everywhere;
> It is in the earth's green covering of grass;
> In the blue serenity of the sky;
> In the reckless exuberance of the spring;
> In the severe abstinence of the gray winter;
> In the living flesh that animates our bodily frame;
> In the perfect poise of the human figure, noble and upright;

In living;
In the exercise of all our powers;
In the acquisition of our knowledge;
In fighting evil.
Joy is there everywhere.

Yes, as the poet says there is a great abundance of joy everywhere in the world. There is innate joy in the universe. It is beyond the dimensions of space and time. It can be found everywhere at any time by anybody. Every moment has the potential to offer plentiful joy. The reality of joy is in the perception of mind. "Without the perception of beauty the wings never spread, the mind lives in shadow, the heart fails," says Nobel-laureate Pearl S. Buck. All of us are endowed with the ability to perceive beauty and joy in life. It is our perception that makes us happy. "Joy seems to be a step beyond happiness," says American journalist Adela Rogers St. Johns. "Happiness is a sort of atmosphere you can live in sometimes when you are lucky. Joy is a light that fills you with hope, faith and love."

Realise, the only reason to be alive is to enjoy it

Man goes after many things in life with a view to enjoying life; but doesn't realise that joy can be found everywhere. Joy is inherent in human existence. "Happiness of the bee and dolphin is to exist," says Capt. Jacques Yves Cousteau, a sub-sea explorer. "For man, it is to know that and wonder at it."

Life is a special gift to you. Former US President Thomas Jefferson says, "The giver of life gave it for happiness not for wretchedness." As American writer Andrew Dunbar puts it – "The gift of happiness belongs to those who unwrap it." We must agree with American writer Rita Mae Brown who says, "I finally figured out, the only reason to be alive is to enjoy it ."

Enjoy the interval

During college days we used to visit theaters to enjoy movies with friends. Soon we discovered that the best part of the movie is the interval. That is the time when we used to enjoy our choicest snacks, pastries and cool drinks. And that was the time we used to have a good chat with friends and enjoy hearty laughs.

After all, our life is an integral part of the 'grand show' called life on earth. If you seriously look at it, it is nothing but the interval between birth and death. " There is no cure for birth or death except to enjoy the interval," says philosopher George Santayana. " Happiness is the only sanction of life; where happiness fails, existence remains a mad lamentable experience." How right he is! Then, why not enjoy this brief interval called life in the same way as we did during college days? Go ahead, do what you will, live the way you want and enjoy life!

Enjoy life while you have it

People everywhere in the world are yearning for peace and happiness in life. But many don't realise that they can enjoy life if they are willing to accept what life offers. "Happiness can only exist in acceptance," as French author Denis de Rougamont puts it.

"Twenty years from now you will be more disappointed by the things you didn't do than by the ones you did do; so throw off the bow lines, sail away from the safe harbour," says American writer Mark Twain. " Catch the trade wind in the sails. Explore. Dream. Discover." Yes, come discover the joy of living! So, "look up, laugh aloud, talk big, keep the colour in your cheek and fire in your eye, adorn your person, maintain your health, your beauty and animal spirits," says British author William Hazlitt. Move forward, with joy in your heart. Enjoy the festival of life. "Dedicate yourself to the good you deserve and desire for yourself, " says motivational speaker Mark Victor Hansen. "Give yourself peace of mind. You deserve to be happy. You deserve delight." All we can say about life is, oh God, let us enjoy it!

Joy and sorrow come together

"Your joy is your sorrow unmasked," says Lebanese philosopher Kahlil Gibran. "Together they come; and when one sits alone with you at your board, remember that the other is asleep up on your bed.... When you are joyous, look deep into your heart and you shall find it is only that which has given you sorrow that is giving you joy. When you are sorrowful, look again in your heart, and you shall see that in truth you are weeping for that which has been your delight."

"Your joy is sorrow unmasked," says French philosopher Rene Descartes. "And the self same well from which your laughter rises was often times filled with your tears." Yes, joy and sorrow come from the same source (you). Welcome and experience both, and enjoy what you like!

On dealing with sorrow

When we hear the agony and grief of people devastated by natural calamities like earthquakes, floods, tornadoes, and volcanic eruptions, we are emotionally moved. When we see thousands of helpless souls hanging on the edge between hope and despair our hearts are overwhelmed by compassion. As caring creatures, we realise the urgency to rescue them and to provide relief. We know that no amount of money or help can ease their sorrow. Yet, as members of great human family we feel for the suffering people and offer help. When we contribute generously for such a great cause we feel a lot of relief. More important is the need to respond sensitively to the emotional needs of the suffering people.

Calamities that cause death seem to trigger compassion in most of us. And we readily join the crowd in trying to help the victims of such disasters. We do the best we can. The aftermath of the 2004 South Asian Tsunami is an example. People of all nations came forward to help the suffering people in whatever way they could. There is joy in expressing compassion and in helping people. As American author Ralph Waldo Emerson says, " It is one of the beautiful compensations of life that no man can sincerely try to help another without helping himself." "Happiness is a product of helping others," says Royden G Derrick, former President of England Leeds Mission. "No man ever finds happiness by thinking about himself. True happiness comes when we lose ourselves in the service of others, when we are merciful to others."

"How agonised we are about how people die. How untroubled we are by how they live." It is indeed a profound statement by P. Sainath, a perceptive journalist, in a recent article in *The Hindu*. Yes, the most unfortunate thing is that our psyche does not seem to be affected by everyday scenes of poverty and suffering, though it expresses occasional sympathy for victims of great calamities. It may be a form of sympathy but certainly not empathy. We have so much of everything in the world, yet so many people are starving and suffering. That is the tragedy of human race on earth.

Don't run away: discover the joy behind challenges in life
Let us not lose hope when we become victims of calamities. "Disappointment in life, is inevitable," says American writer Anna Robertson Brown. "Pain is the common lot. Sorrow is not given to us alone that we may mourn. It is given us, that having felt, suffered, wept, we may be able to understand love, bless."

It is natural that we crave for sympathy, but what we really want in such desperate circumstances is not sympathy or charity but genuine help–to help ourselves. Remember, the words of Nobel laureate Dag Hammarskjold: "Life only demands from you the strength you possess. Only one feat is possible—not to have run away." No problem is mightier than your courage! Come what may, be ready to face it; your courage will certainly make you 'the last man standing.'

Cry if you will : relief you get later is a hidden joy
We are always between tears and laughter, meeting crises big and small. Life is always like that. Whenever we see suffering or death sympathetic vibrations trigger emotional outbursts in all of us. Sometimes we hesitate to express our feelings in public, but we don't have to. Don't struggle to control your emotions; cry, if the occasion calls for it. Let your tears run their stream; let them drain your pain. It will surely lift the burden on your heart and lighten the strain on your mind. You will definitely heave a sigh of relief—you know it. The relief that follows is the wonderful reward you can ever get. In fact, it's another form of joy behind tears! "One kind of happiness is to know exactly at what point to be miserable," says French author Francois de la Rouchefoucauld.

Focus on happy elements in your life. If you can't see the bright side, stop grumbling. Polish the dull side. It will help dilute or decrease the impact of negative elements. By bringing in the positives into the light you can build on them a beautiful edifice of your life. Make sure you look for the good in circumstances and people to help keep positive. Even in sadness you can find joy. As British poet PB Shelly puts it, "Our sweetest thoughts are those that tell of saddest things." Realise, that happiness comes from being a little uncomfortable as often as possible, so you are always learning and growing.

What is the use of worrying? It never was worthwhile. "Waste not fresh tears over old griefs," advises Greek philosopher Euripides. It is patently unfair to be sorrowful in a world that offers plenty of joys. So pack up your troubles in an old kit bag. And smile, smile, smile. Assure your smiles even in the darkest hour of sorrow.

We need sorrow to appreciate joy

"Our sense of delight is in a great measure comparative," says British author Samuel Johnson, " and arises at once from the sensations which we feel, and those which we remember: thus ease after torment is pleasure for a time, and we are very agreeably recreated when the body, chilled with the weather, is gradually recovering its tepidity; but the joy ceases when we have forgotten the cold; we must fall below ease again if we desire to rise above it, and purchase new facility by voluntary pain."

"Even a happy life cannot be without a measure of darkness," says the Austrian psychiatrist Carl Jung; "and the word 'happy' would lose its meaning if it were not balanced by sadness. It is far better to take things as they come along with patience and equanimity." Yes, just as we must feel the cold to appreciate warmth, taste savories to appreciate sweets, we must experience sorrow to appreciate joy.

"The thing to remember is that, in joy and sorrow alike, life is precious," says American author Ardis Whitman (Reader's Digest, April '86). " And perhaps we never have the need to ask of it more than this: that it gives us a chance to be what we can be; experience what we can experience; and love what we can love."

Sharing increases joy, reduces sorrow

We all know that by sharing joyful moments with family members and friends we virtually distribute happiness. Sharing joy, in fact, is sharing life with others. On the other hand, by sharing our woes with our close friends and relatives we get a sigh of relief that lightens the burden on our hearts. Consider how beautifully this wonderful phenomenon is captured by a Swedish proverb: "Shared joy is double joy, shared sorrow is half sorrow."

Cultivate happy–to-be-alive attitudes
The only person who can bring happiness in your life is you. Essentially happiness stems from your present attitude. As American journalist Hugh Downs puts it, "A happy person is not a person in a set of circumstances, but rather a person with a set of attitudes." Unless you develop happy-to-be-alive attitudes you can never be happy. "If we cannot live as to be happy, let us at least live so as to deserve to be happy," says British philosopher Immanuel Kant.

Choose to be happy
"What we call secret of happiness is no more than a secret of our willingness to choose life," says Dr. Felice Leonard Buscaglia. You can choose to think and feel as you desire. You can make yourself happy or miserable—it is the same amount of effort. The most sensible commitment you can make in the world is to be happy. Happiness comes from conscious choice not chance. Nobel laureate Aleksander Solzhenitsyn says, "It is not the level of prosperity that makes for happiness but the kinship of heart to heart and the way we look at the world. Both attributes are within our power, so that a man is happy so long as he chooses to be happy; and no one can stop him."

Find ecstasy in joyful life
This life of ours is but a short sojourn. It is going to end very soon, we know. But why think about it when you are alive and kicking? Think about your life. Remember no joy is greater than the supreme joy of living. Excite your senses, exhilarate your soul, immerse yourself with this highest joy. "Find ecstasy in life; mere sense of living is joy enough," says Emily Elizabeth Dickinson, the New England mystic and poet. She exhorts, "The soul should always stand ajar ready to welcome ecstatic experience." What a wonderful message!

Magic of ordinary days: discover hidden joys

Pause for a while to enjoy life

There we go again, always thinking of the next moment in life forgetting the entertaining fare provided by the present moments. "Plenty of people miss their share of happiness not because they never found it; but because they didn't stop to enjoy it," points out Nobel laureate William Faulkner. So, take a fresh look at your life and appreciate the wonder hidden in tiny moments—small, basic everyday moments can offer joy. See what blissful moments of joy and happiness you may be missing. As French surrealist Guillaume Apollinaire says, "Now and then it is good to pause in our pursuit of happiness and just be happy."

Enjoy simple joys before you look for ecstasy

Psychologist Norbert Schwarz and his colleagues at the University of Michigan, reported in an article published in *Science*, that it is not money but the simplest of the routine activities that determine how happy we are in our daily life, they hold the key to our happiness. The researchers analysed questionnaires from a convenient sample of 909 working women and found that activities such as intimate relations, socialising, relaxing, eating, exercising, and watching TV were among the most enjoyable activities.

"The art of being happy lies in the power of extracting happiness from common things," says Clergyman Henry Ward Beacher. "Happiness is the art of making a banquet of those flowers within reach," says American author Bob Goddard. Any small thing around can please us and make us happy. " For most part of life, nothing wonderful happens," says TV commentator Andy Rooney. "If you do enjoy getting up and working and finishing your work and sitting down to meal with family and friends , then the chances are you're going to be happy. If someone bases his or her happiness on major events like a great job, a flawless happy marriage or a trip to Paris, that person isn't going to be happy much of the time. If, on the other hand, happiness depends on a good breakfast, flowers in the yard, a drink or nap, then we are more likely to live with quite a bit of happiness."

So, don't look for happiness in glitzy things that cost you a fortune. Joy and delight can be found in such simple things that you can find everywhere, if only you look for them. In "The Time to be Happy" (*Reader's Digest,* Aug.'66) American writer Elizabeth Starr Hill says, "Many seemingly humdrum aspects of everyday living can give us pleasure if we but take the time to contemplate them: the comforting tick of the clock, the colours of flowers, the smell of freshly brewed coffee, relaxation of hot bath, drifting off to sleep when tired, and the refreshed awakening."

In *Quest for Freedom,* Surjit Singh Barnala, former Governor of Tamilnadu, describes how he longed to have the thrill of 'being with real people' again; obviously he was fed up with the protocols of the office of Governor. Before day break he was sitting in a truck, with a blackened beard, as Kartar Singh bound for Indore. He even travelled 'without an itinerary' to Ajanta and Ellora caves and then to Lucknow. " It was like being on the first floor of a moving house," he reminisced. In a chapter titled 'simple joys' he recounts his wandering through the bazaar, visit to the fair, stay in a hut with a *banjara,* and so on. He says, " the roadside *dhabas* serve better food than most five-star hotels and at one-fiftieth price. The service is normally superlative." That is how he describes how one can find joy even in most depressing circumstances.

"No body is ever happy 24 hours a day, seven days a week," says Marriage Counsellor James E Faust. "Rather than thinking in terms of a day, we perhaps need to snatch happiness in little pieces, learning to recognise the elements of happiness and then treasuring them while they last." Happiness looks so small when you hold it in your hands; just let it go once, you will realise how precious it is.

Be Grateful for What Life Offers

"Happiness itself is a form of gratitude", says American author Joseph Wood Krutch. Remember, contentment is the root of happiness. Be content with what life offers you; and be happy with what you have.

"Thanks are highest form of thought, and that gratitude is happiness doubled by wonder," says American author Gilbert Keith Chesterton. So, as French writer Marcel Proust says, "Let us be grateful to people who make us happy; they are the charming gardeners who make our souls blossom." Remember, thankfulness and gratitude are the hallmarks of a grateful heart.

Celebrate Your Life

The greatest reason to be happy is life itself

German philosopher Franz Kafka says, "We need an ice axe to break the frozen sea within us." In this context American writer George Kent says, "The best axe is a shock of happiness," (*Reader's Digest*, July '66). Let me give you an example: The happiest thing in anybody's life is the *life* in the body! It is indeed surprising when we realise its blissful presence. We know life itself is the greatest reason to be happy. *Taking birth as a human being* is a great blessing. The awareness of *being alive* is a greater joy ; and the feeling that we are *still alive* to enjoy life for some more time is the greatest joy in the world. No joy is comparable to the supreme joy of living, because all the joys in the world become available only when you are alive! This is because you still have some more time left that allows you to make the best of remaining life. That is good enough reason to celebrate living!

We know the life of a flower is very short; yet we love to enjoy its beauty and fragrance. Likewise our life does not last forever. But in spite of its impermanence, we can still enjoy life with all its dreams, desires, hopes, promises and joys. " We are here for a spell; get all the good laughs you can," says American humorist Will Rogers. Celebrate life with fun and make merry. There is no time like our life-time to rejoice and enjoy.

Life is not a dress rehearsal where you can afford to falter and correct later. Yes, we are talking about your life—the real life, where you don't get a second chance. If you love it you can enjoy it. But then you have a choice ; you can love it or leave it. Like driving a car, living your life can be fun if you have passion for it. Love it, live it, rock it, feel it, smell it, taste it. Any experience can be exciting, pleasurable and joyful. Abundance of joy exists in life in various forms. It is all yours, if only you are willing to discover it.

Rejoice, you are still alive!
We are blessed with life, but for once. No second take here! Be happy for the precious life of a human being. Count your blessings, because *you are still alive.* If you can discover this truth, it will be like a 'baptism of fire.' You will have the 'born again' experience with your spirit bubbling inside. Fill yourself with its fizz—the *joy of living*. Once you realise that it is the greatest joy in life, other joys will follow. Enjoy your life!

"The way to love anything, is to realise that it might be lost," says American author Gilbert Keith Chesterton. You have to learn to love your life, because in all certainty it will be lost—any time from now. Some more time seems to have been still left to allow you to live—I mean, to let you live joyfully. You have three great reasons to rejoice and be happy! First, you are still *alive!* Second, it allows you to be joyful. Third, you can experience the *joy of living*. Just this feeling of being alive, in itself, is quite delightful. So, be joyful as long as the life permits you! Life is indeed a many splendoured thing in the world.

Celebrate life with fellow beings
It is impossible to ignore the joy of living, because you are not going to live again. It is worth celebrating. Come let's party, let's enjoy life. "Make every day a holiday and celebrate just living," exhorts American poet Amanda Bradley.

Let us make our life-time a celebration time. So, go ahead—full throttle; enjoy life, its all yours. Believe in yourself, your faith, your success, your love and your hope. Indulge in what you wish, within the expanse of your own morals and lead a joyful life. Share your joy with fellow beings, light up the world.

Love your life: make everyday a joy to live!
Nobel laureate Rabindranath Tagore wrote in *Personality*:

> "Let us live. Let us have the true joy of life, which is the joy of the poet in pouring himself out in his poem. Let us express our infinity in everything around us, in works we do, in things we use, in men with whom we deal, in the enjoyment of the world with which we are surrounded. Let our soul permeate our surroundings and create itself in all things, and show its fullness, by fulfilling the needs of all times. This life of ours has been filled with gifts of the divine giver. The stars have sung to it, it has been blessed with the daily blessing of the morning light, the fruits have been sweet to it, and the earth has spread its carpet of grass so that it may have its rest. And let it like an instrument fully break out in the music of its soul in response to the touch of the infinite soul."

Life is indeed pregnant with joy, full of it, in various forms. Remember, it's all yours, if you so desire. Love to live joyfully and enjoy every moment of your life. Do whatever you like. See its formless beauty and admire its timeless grace. Listen to its lilting tunes and dance to its exotic music. Breathe its pleasing fragrance and enjoy its enlivening spirits. Lick its sweet honey and drink its life-giving nectar. Taste its heavenly *manna* and relish its delicious fruits. Feel its softness and enjoy its sensuality. Above all, experience its sparkling liveliness and appreciate its enduring promises. Don't forget to live it to the full and to the end of your heart's content. Realise that the only reason to live is to enjoy it.

Soon you will have gone forever. But you don't have to worry, there is plenty of time to be dead! Since you have some more time to enjoy life, it is wise to make the best of your remaining life. Try to be happy and enjoy life as long as you live! "Each day a basic goal must be your feeling that you deserve to enjoy, whether you are a millionaire or a pauper," says Maxwell Maltz, the psycho-cybernetics guru. Joyful living today means joyful *day* today. Then another good day. And another good day. One day at a time. You add up a succession of joyful days—and you have a joyful life. Listen to the counsel of inspirational speaker Dr. Norman Vincent Peale: "Start each day by affirming peaceful, contented happy attitudes and your days will tend to be pleasant and successful." Love your life. Get the feel of its abundance, its blessings, its happiness, its joy. Make every day a joy to live.

So long my friend! Enjoy the festival of life!

References

Alda, Alan, "Dig into the World", *Reader's Digest*, December 1981.
Amos, Wayne, "Eternity's Sunrise", *Reader's Digest*, April 1965.
Bardwick, Judith M. *Seeking the Calm in the Storm: Managing Chaos in Your Business Life*. Prentice Hall, 2002.
Barnala, Surjit Singh. *Quest for Freedom*. Natraj Publishers, Dehradun, 2004.
Barnard, Christiaan N, "In Celebration of Being Alive", *Reader's Digest*, Dec. 1980.
Beach, Leslie R, and Elton L Clark. *Psychology in Business*, McGraw Hill, New York 1959.
Brody, Jane, "Become a 'Type B.'" *Reader's Digest*, Feb. 1982.
   Brody, Jane. 'Keep Fit—For life', *Reader's Digest*, January 1991.
Brower, Charles, "How to Be a Failure", *Reader's Digest*, Feb. 1966.
Buchan, James, *Frozen Desire: The Meaning of Money*. Farrar Straus Giroux, New York 1997.
Buck, Pearl .S, "Joy of Children", *Reader's Digest*, November, 1965.
Burgess, Gilett, "The Delightful Game of Conversation", *Reader's Digest*, July 1967.
Burns, Dr. David, "Aim for Success not Perfection", *Reader's Digest*, October, 1985.
Callwood, June, "The One Sure Way to Happiness", *Reader's Digest*, January 1965.
Campion, Nardi Reeder, "What Really Is Worthwhile" *Reader's Digest*, 19 May 1995.
Carnegie, Dale, "How to Win Friends and Influence People", *Reader's Digest*, April 1977.
Cheung, Theresa. *Coffee Wisdom: 7 Finely Ground Principles for Living Full Bodied Life*. Red wheel / Weiser, 2003.
Chimpy, James and Nitin Nohria, *The Arc of Ambition*.
Clarkson, Petruska. *How to Overcome Your Secret Fear of Failure*, Magna Publishing Co, 2005.
Covey, Stephen R. *The Seven Habits of Highly Effective People*, Simon & Schuster, New York 1989.
Culhane, John. "Keep a Happiness Calendar" *Reader's Digest*, June 1987.
Dobson, James. "The Greatest Gift You Can Give to Your Child", *Reader's Digest*, June 1988.

Dukas, Helen and Banesh Hoffman. "Yours Sincerely, Albert Einstein" *Reader's Digest*, October 1979.
Durant, Will. "Man is Wiser Than Any Man" *Reader's Digest*, March 1969.
Dyer, Wayne. "Happiness—It's Only Natural", *Reader's Digest*, June 1978.
Farrel, Larry C. *Getting Entrepreneurial*, Wiley.
Flocker, Michael. *The New Hedonism Handbook: Master the Lost Art of Leisure and Pleasure*, Da Capo Press, 2004.
Frankl, Dr. Victor E. *Man's Search for Meaning*, Pocket books 1997.
Frazier, John. 'Breathe Right and Stay Well', *Reader's Digest*, April 1966.
Gallup, Jr. George, Alec Gallup and William Proctor. "What Successful People Have in Common", *Reader's Digest*, Nov. 1987.
Gibran, Kahlil. *The Prophet*, Alfred Knoff, Pocket edition, 1995.
Hamilton, Donald L., *Mind of Mankind*, Sunir Press, 1996.
Hill, Elizabeth Starr, "The Time to Be Happy", *Reader's Digest*, August 1966.
Hunt, Morton. "Seven Secrets of Peak Performers" *Reader's Digest*, November 1982.
Janeway, Elizabeth, "The Time of Your Life", *Reader's Digest*, April 1966.
James, William, "Your Secret Strength", *Reader's Digest*, April 1995.
Kalidasa. *The Ritusamhara of Kalidasa: New Translation of Sanskrit Classic*. Dialogue Publishers, Calcutta, 1970.
Kent, George, 'Shocks of Happiness', *Reader's Digest*, July 1966.
Kiester, Jr., Edwin and Sally Valente Kiester. "Bring Fun Back to Your Marriage", *Reader's Digest*, May 1989.
Kennedy, Diane, *Loopholes of the Rich*, John Wiley and Sons, 2004.
Kozicki, Stephen, *The Creative Negotiator*, Gover Pub Co 1994.
Landers, Ann, "Coping With Crisis", *Reader's Digest*, April 1981.
Layard, Richard, *Happiness: Lessons From a New Science*.
Lim, Billi. PS, *Dare to Fail*, Hardknocks Factory, 1996.
Lindstrom, Aletha Jane. "Care a Little, Care a Lot", *Reader's Digest*, March 1981.
Maltz, Maxwell, *Creative Living Today*, Pocket Books, New York, 1967.
Mayo, Stacy. *I Can't Believe I Get Paid to Do This*.
McKenna, Colleen. *Powerful Communication Skills*, Magna Publishing Co, 2005.
Michelmore, Peter. "Emotions Do Rule Our Health", *Reader's Digest*, June 1984.
Miller, James Nathan. "The Art of Intelligent Listening", *Reader's Digest*, November, 1965.
Morgan, Clifford T, Richard A. King, John R. Weise, et al. *Introduction to Psychology*, McGraw Hill 1986.
Mosley, Jean Bell. "Take It from the Here and Now", *Reader's Digest*, Sept. 1968.

Osgood, Charles E, G.J. Suci and P.H. Tannenbaum. *The Measurement of Meaning,* Urbana. University of Illinois Press, 1957.
Osho, *The Body Mind Balancing,* St. Martin's Griffin, 2005.
Osho, *Meditation: The Art of Ecstasy,* Tao Publishing Co, 2005.
Oslie, Pamala, *Make Your Dreams Come True.* Magna Publishing Co, 2005.
Peale, Dr.Norman Vincent, "Make Your Dreams Come True", *Reader's Digest,* Dec.1983.
Pierce, Ponchitta, "Three Steps to Confidence", *Reader's Digest,* August 1976.
Prather, Hugh. *Shining Through: Switch Your Life and Ground Your Self in Happiness,* Conari Press 2004.
Rather, Dan, "How to Handle Pressure", *Reader's Digest,* March, 1984.
Seligman, Martin EP. *Authentic Happiness: Using the New Positive Psychology For Lasting Fulfillment.* Free Press, New York, 2002.
Selye, Hans *interviewed* by Laurence Cherry. 'Straight Talk About Stress', *Reader's Digest,* Dec. 1982.
Sethi, Geet. *Success vs Joy.* 20:20 Media, New Delhi, 2004.
Sheinfeld, Robert. *The Invisible Path to Success.* Magna Publishing Co, 2005.
Singer, Jerome. "Don't Be Afraid to Daydream", *Reader's Digest,* Oct. 1976.
Smith, Philip. 'Breathe Your Troubles Away', *Reader's Digest,* Feb. 1982.
Sussman, Vic. 'Don't Fear Failure', *Reader's Digest,* Jan. 1991.
Tagore, Rabindranath, *Personality: Lectures Delivered in America,* MacMillan, London,1926.
Tam, Marilyin, *How to Use What You Have to Get What You Want.* Magna Publishing Co. 2005.
Tessina, Tina B, *It Ends With You: Grow Up and Out of Dysfunction,* Newpage Books, 2003.
Thoreau, Henry David, "Simplify, Simplify!", *Reader's Digest,* May 1978.
Wren, PC and H. Martin. *High School English Grammar and Composition.* S. Chand & Co, New Delhi.
Whitman, Ardis, "Five Enduring Values for Your Child", *Reader's Digest,* Dec. 1981.
Whitman, Ardis, "Secret Joys of Solitude", *Reader's Digest,* Nov. 1983.
Whitman, Ardis, "The Awesome Power to Be Ourselves", *Reader's Digest,* July 1983.
Whitman, Ardis, "Resources to Last a Life Time", *Reader's Digest,* April 1986.
Yager, Jan, *When Friendship Hurts,* Fireside 2002.
Young, Steve, *Great Failures of the Extremely Successful: Mistakes, Adversity, Failures and Other Stepping Stones for Success,* Tallfellow Press 2002.
Zakich, Rhea, "Simple Secrets of Family Communication', *Reader's Digest,* Feb. 1987.